RICHMOND PARK
The Walker's Historical Guide

by
David McDowall

with sketch maps and line drawings by
Angela Kidner

COVER: *Richmond Park* by Sharland, 1911

First published 1996 by David McDowall
31 Cambrian Road, Richmond, Surrey TW10 6JQ

© David McDowall 1996

The right of David McDowall to be identified as the author of this work has been
asserted by him in accordance with the Copyright, Design and Patents Act 1988

British Library Cataloguing in Publication Data
A catalogue record for this book is available from the British Library

ISBN 0 9527847 0 X

Designed and typeset in Monotype Abadi and ITC Oficina by Peter Moore
Produced by Graham Laird, Berndale Limited, Ashtead, Surrey
Printed by Headley Brothers Ltd, Ashford, Kent

Contents

Maps

Illustrations

Acknowledgements

I have had a lot of help in putting this book together. First, I am indebted to those who have already written on the park. Most of this is in published form:

Anon, *Two Historical Accounts of the Making of the new Forest in Hampshire and Richmond New Park in Surrey* (London, 1751)

'A Resident' (J. Lucas), *A History of Richmond New Park* (London, 1877)

Michael Baxter Brown, *Richmond Park: The History of a Royal Deer Park* (London, 1985)

Beresford Chancellor, *The History and Antiquities of Richmond, Kew, Petersham and Ham* (Richmond, 1894)

John Cloake, *Richmond Past* (London 1992)

John Cloake, *Palaces and Parks of Richmond and Kew* vols I and II (Chichester, 1995, 1996).

C.L. Collenette, *A History of Richmond Park* (London 1937, reprinted 1971)

Pamela Fletcher Jones, *Richmond Park – a portrait of a Royal Playground* (London and Chichester, 1972, reprinted 1883)

Thomas Nelson, *Richmond Park: Extracts from the Records of Parliament and of the Corporation of London* (London, 1883)

Coryn de Vere, *Handbook of Richmond Park* (London, 1909).

In addition, however, I owe a particular debt to the survey carried out by Dr Tom Greeves on behalf of the Royal Parks, for the identification of prehistoric and medieval features described in the first four walks of this book. His *Richmond Park, London: Archaeological Survey* (The Royal Parks, unpublished mimeograph, London 1992) may, like the books listed above, be consulted in the Local Studies Room of Richmond Public Library.

His findings have been indispensible to the first three walks of this book, and also valuable for the identification of earthworks elsewhere.

I owe a great debt to the generosity and unrivalled knowledge of John Cloake, Richmond's outstanding local historian. He kindly showed me the manuscript of his second volume of *Palaces and Parks of Richmond and Kew* before its publication and also carefully read my manuscript catching numerous errors of fact and judgment. To him I owe great thanks. At the Local Studies Collection, Richmond Public Library, Jane Baxter and her colleagues have been always extraordinarily efficient and helpful, locating materials in the collection and kindly supplying most of the illustrations. The Museum of London also kindly allowed me to examine a photograph of the original enclosure map of Nicholas Lane. R.G.Phillip kindly allowed me to quote from F.D.Ommaney's *The House in the Park* and Routledge kindly allowed me to quote from *The Autobiography of Bertrand Russell* (George Allen and Unwin Ltd, 1967) vol.i, pp.13,30. In the park itself I have had nothing but courtesy and helpfulness from its staff, notably Mike Fitt, Geoffrey Brock, Dave Smith, Jane Braham, Dick Farr and Mike Lewis, who have shared their knowledge and tried to correct my misunderstandings. Thanks, too, to my wife, Elizabeth, for reading the text, and checking for inadequate explanations, *non sequitors* and typographical errors. She has encouraged me throughout.

I owe a major double debt to Angela and Patrick Kidner. They doggedly tested each walk regardless of the weather, giving me both encouragement and comments in perfect measure. In addition Angela walked the ground yet again to draw the sketch maps, and drew her impressions of the appearance of pre-enclosure buildings from the very scanty indications on the original enclosure map of Nicholas Lane and from research into late medieval to early Jacobean buildings in Surrey. She has given this book a very special quality and I am greatly indebted to her.

THE ILLUSTRATIONS

I am most grateful to the London Transport Museum for permission to use Sharland's *Richmond Park*, 1911, as the cover illustration, and to the London Borough of Richmond upon Thames Local Studies Collection for the provision of all the illustrations, with the exception of Angela Kidner's line drawings of buildings enclosed by Charles I and her sketch maps.

Richmond Park: overview

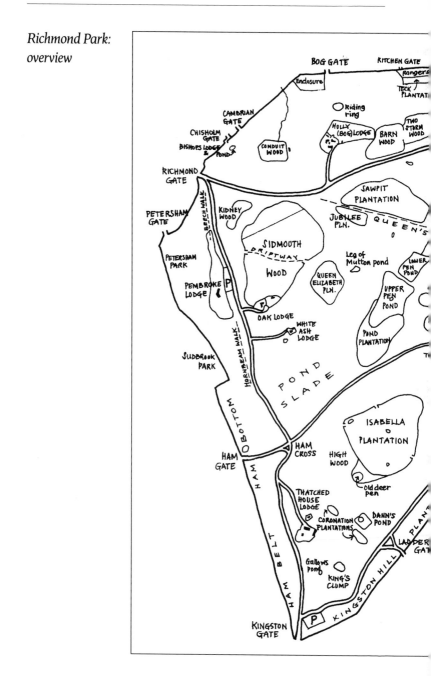

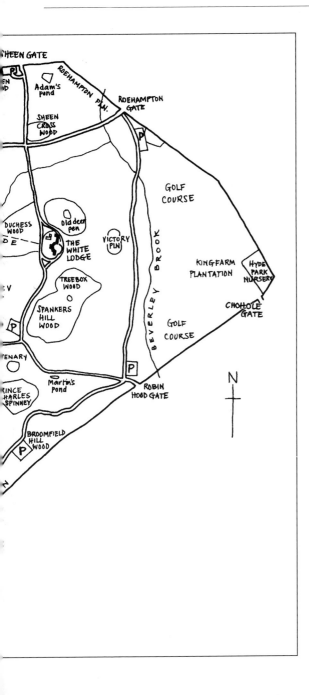

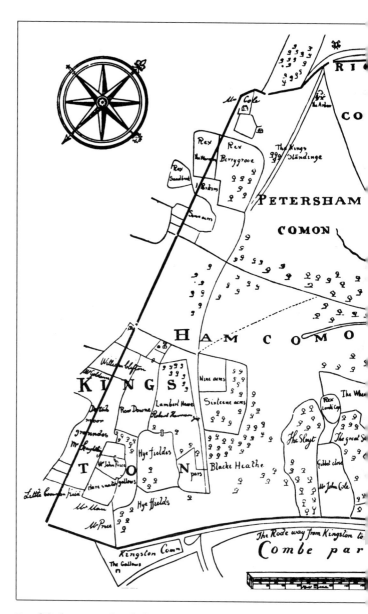

Simplified version of Nicholas Lane's Enclosure Map 1632-37.
(Note that the compass orientation is different from the sketch maps in this book.)

Introduction

Richmond Park is one of the largest enclosed parks in Britain, over 2,500 acres in size. It is also the least disturbed expanse of land in the Greater London area with prehistoric, medieval as well as more modern traces of human activity.

This is because Charles I enclosed the land as a royal hunting park between 1632 and 1637. Very little ground disturbance has happened since then, except during the two world wars. Consequently visible traces of previous land use may be found in many parts of the park, a real rarity in south eastern England.

This guide is about finding and enjoying traces of the past uses to which this incomparable part of London has been put. It is intended as a walking companion, both for those who already habitually use the park, but also for newcomers who wish to enjoy the more concealed delights the park has to offer. There are no earth shattering revelations, and the features described are almost invariably subtle but distinct enough that with imagination one can reconstruct in the mind's eye what things may have looked like. Features on the first three walks are sufficiently subtle that the walks should only be undertaken in the period mid-December to May, when ground features are not obscured by bracken and other cover. Some features may seem unprepossessing, but if your experience is like mine, the more you walk the park the more pleasure they will give and your feeling for the park will, I hope, be enriched in the process. The guide is organised as a series of walks for those who like a set itinerary or who may be unfamiliar with the park's geography. For that reason most set walks commence from a car park. However, I hope many walkers will know exactly where many of the sites mentioned in the text are located, choose their own routes and feel no need slavishly to adhere to the walks as prescribed. However, I have discovered that, having thought I knew the park rather well, one has a tendency only to walk favoured routes. It is a secondary intention, therefore, to lure walkers into exploring parts of the park they know only vaguely. I have appended notes on the woods, deer, birds and ponds as casual references to satisfy your curiosity as you walk.

Walks are illustrated where necessary with sketch maps, and with a reference sketch map of the whole park on page 10. Numbers in brackets in the text indicate that the features to which they refer may be located on the relevant sketch map.

It is my hope and purpose that your appreciation of this wonderful and unique landscape will slowly be transformed through this book, as it was for me while researching it.

Finally, this guide does not belong on a bookshelf. If it doesn't live in a coat pocket and become rapidly dog-eared, I shall have failed.

David McDowall
Richmond, May 1996

1 *The Prehistoric and ancient sites*

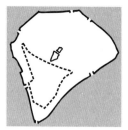

(7km/2.5 hours)

ONLY UNDERTAKE THIS WALK BETWEEN MID-DECEMBER AND MAY WHEN GROUND COVER IS MINIMAL

Start: Pembroke Lodge car park.
Please note that dogs are not admitted into Pembroke Lodge grounds.

Proceed northwards (i.e in the direction of Richmond Gate) from the car park, following the perimeter fence of Pembroke Lodge, ignore the first pedestrian entrance (50m) and enter the Pembroke Lodge estate by its northern gate (350m approx from the car park). Pass through the 'Laburnum Walk' and you find yourself facing King Henry VIII's Mound (1), see map on p.17.

This is the highest point in the park. Writing in 1835, Edward Jesse, Deputy Surveyor of the Royal Parks (see Walk No. 7), was probably the first to recognize the likely existence of prehistoric barrows. This is what he says:

> 'This mound has long been celebrated as the spot on which Henry the Eighth stood to watch the going up of a rocket to assure him that the death of Anne Boleyn would enable him to marry Lady Jane Seymour. This is the tradition of the park, and it has been handed down from father to son by several park-keepers. There can be no doubt but that this mound was formerly a British barrow. It has been opened, and a considerable deposit of ashes was found in the centre of it.'

Alas, it is known that Henry VIII spent that evening of 19 May 1536, the day of Anne's execution, in Wiltshire. Euphoria has its limits and a 60-mile ride surely exceeds them, even for a man just freed of a troublesome wife. But it makes a good story, and the name is at least 250 years old and possibly older. In 1637 it was called 'the King's Standinge', and may have been a vantage point for falconry in the valley below. But Jesse was almost certainly right in identifying it as a prehistoric burial mound, although at some stage it lost its conical top.

It is worth remembering that the first (Neolithic) cultivators probably arrived in Britain in about 3500BC. These were apparently the first people to keep animals, for example pigs, and to use a light plough, skills they brought from continental Europe. They did not yet live in villages, but in scattered individual homesteads, small rectangular houses made of wattle (interlaced branches) and daub (a mixture of animal dung and straw), roofed with turf or rushes. Before then humans had lived by hunting and foraging.

It was the people of this new farming culture that first constructed barrows in which to bury their dead. The suspected barrows in the park date any time from about 3000BC to the period when barrow construction petered out, around 900BC. This may seem very imprecise, but until they are excavated even their status as barrows must remain in some doubt.

We do know, however, without any doubt at all that at least one Late Bronze Age settlement existed in the park. Pottery sherds (c. 900BC) have been found in the gravel north of Holly (Bog) Lodge, just west of the riding ring, and one may expect this settlement to have had predecessors (discussed later). The rabbits that abound here still kick up the occasional small sherd.

Having enjoyed the view across the Thames valley, look in the opposite direction through the 'window'. On a clear day you will see St Paul's Cathedral beautifully framed by the cutting through Sidmouth Wood. The avenue of sweet chestnuts running up to the cutting marks the alignment of a circular and probably prehistoric earthwork adjacent to and on the eastern side of the horse ride (100m away – it is noticeable because of the bracken growing in it) and another probable barrow, 'Oliver's Mound', which once stood in the Sidmouth Wood cutting but which was destroyed by gravel diggers in 1834. The skeletons they found at the time are unlikely to have been prehistoric on account of the acidity of the soil. However, the alignment of these three supposedly pre-historic features is intriguing, and may constitute a 'ley line' (these alignments, first noticed in the 1920s, may have marked ancient routes or had some astronomical significance, but are still treated with caution or scepticism by archaeologists).

The avenue of trees is itself old by our standards. We may not know what tree species was used, but the avenue certainly existed at the beginning of the eighteenth century, as may be seen on Kip's illustration of Petersham Park dated 1708 (p.46).

(Oliver's Mound was supposedly named after Oliver Cromwell, but he came no closer than Ham, in November 1647. It may have been named after him by a grateful City of London Corporation which was granted the park during the Commonwealth, 1649-60.)

Proceed southwards through Pembroke Lodge grounds, passing along the rear of the Lodge itself, and keeping straight to go out of the Lodge grounds at the wicket gate at the southernmost end of the grounds. Walk along the informal footpath that follows the escarpment (you will notice the more formal Hornbeam Walk running parallel on your left) for approximately 600m. Do not stray from the escarpment edge.

Walking along the escarpment is a good moment to consider the dramatic changes that happened to the landscape of the park in prehistoric times as a result of climate and geology. We are speaking of an enormous time span, for human interest starts

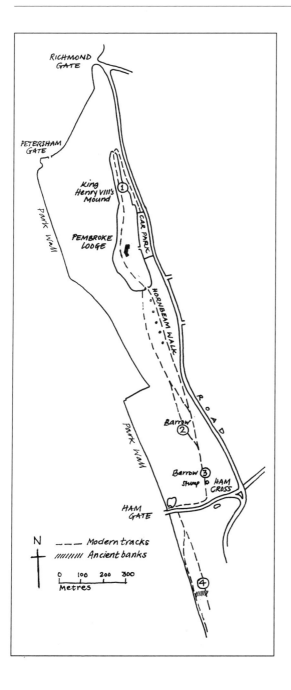

almost half a million years ago.

The underlying geological structure of the park is predominantly London Clay, but with three main bands of sandy/ gravelly deposits forming high ground, most obviously the escarpment from Richmond Gate to Kingston Hill which you are now following; and also the area north of Holly (Bog) Lodge, the high ground around White Lodge, Spankers Hill, the Isabella Plantation, the north west side of the Pen Ponds, and near East Sheen Gate.

These sandy gravel areas are the result of fluvio-glacial deposits on top of the London Clay during what is known as the great interglacial period, approximately 240,000 - 430,000 years ago. At its furthest extent the ice-cap covered the Midlands and almost reached the Thames. During warmer phases, for complex reasons, the sea level rose higher than it is today. During the great interglacial period the sea level was about 30m higher, and during the two subsequent interglacial periods, about 20m and 8m respectively above the level today. Rivers of melted glacier deposited large quantities of gravel on the landscape. Hence there are 'terraces' of gravelly deposits relating to successive interglacial periods. These deposits proved less susceptible to erosion than London Clay, hence it became the high ground.

Virtually all prehistoric artefacts found in the park have, predictably, been found on the gravel 'terraces' left by fluvio-glacial action, not on the clay. Since the Thames and its feeders changed course during these warmer phases, they left many areas of gravel deposit in the London area – for example Hampstead Heath – and also cut deep channels through the clay bed.

It was during these warmer phases that early hominids found Britain relatively tolerable and lived here. At the time of Boxgrove Man, 500,000 years ago, the climate seems to have been warmer than today, with lions and rhinoceroses roaming the landscape. After the next ice age, a period from approximately 470,000 to

430,000 years ago, the climate was often as inhospitable as that today in the Arctic Circle, with a similar tundra landscape. Consequently, humans inhabited the warmer drier sandy gravelly areas in preference to the lower, wetter clay areas.

The oldest artefacts found in the park (on high ground near the White Lodge) are flint tools of the Paleolithic period, about 400,000 years ago, during the Great Interglacial Period. They probably belonged to *homo erectus*, an early hominid predator, thought to be our direct ancestor. During the next interglacial period, 150,000 years ago, fallow deer roamed Britain before disappearing with the last ice age.

More recent flints from the Mesolithic period, that is the period between the end of the last ice age about 8300BC and before the introduction of farming in about 3500BC, have been found at a lower level, around Ham Dip, Dann's Pond and the Pen Ponds. In 1953 a fine flint axe of about 5000-4000BC was found in the Isabella Plantation, and is now on display in the Richmond Museum. These implements belonged to modern humankind (*homo sapiens sapiens*).

For the first time we can imagine the scene. From about 8000BC the climate was almost as warm as today. The open tundra had given way to trees. The landscape and flora of the park by now were probably recognizably similar to today. First came birch (still present in the park), then pine, hazel and eventually forests, mainly oak but also with elm and lime trees. The animal population changed. Wild horses, mammoth, elk and bison declined or disappeared and were replaced by more familiar woodland animals: red deer, wild ox, boar, badgers, foxes and hedgehogs. People hunted them with flint-tipped spears, and killed and skinned them with flint knives and scrapers.

In about 6500BC, during this Mesolithic period, the land link with the continent was submerged (thank heavens, an island race at last). By now wood was a central material of human culture, used to make axe hafts, harpoon and spear shafts, and also wattle fencing, no doubt very similar to that still used today. They presumably knew about coppicing (the cultivation of small trees like hazels, the shoots of which are regularly cut to provide poles, staves, handles, wattle, etc.). They had also learnt how to use antler and bone as tools. (So had Boxgrove Man half a million years earlier, but it is unclear whether intervening hominid species had these skills.)

When you have walked about 500m from Pembroke Lodge grounds the path dips and then rises, you should see a large trunked oak tree 20 paces on your left, known as John Martin's oak (after a 19th century romantic artist who painted it), standing on what is probably a small prehistoric mound. The tree is worth inspecting since the trunk is more massive than it initially seems. Resume the path and you will see that it rises over a distinct mound with an oak growing out of it about 40m ahead.

This is probably a barrow (2). It was excavated in the early nineteenth century, and according to Jesse, broken pottery and ash deposits found. The pottery might have told us the approximate date of the barrow. When one bears in mind the amount of work involved in the construction of barrows it is difficult to believe that they are simply graves in the modern sense. Almost certainly they also held symbolic power, possibly representing the power of dead ancestors, and possibly used as focal points for social, political or economic transactions.

Another possible barrow (3), easy to locate but very much more difficult to spot lies 300m south, and is lost in the bracken except during January-April. To find it continue the same path until you are about 20 paces from a large 6' tall oak stump marking the end of the path. The suspected barrow is on your right, identifiable by two hawthorns and an oak growing on top of it.

However, one must be cautious. Until these barrows are excavated, we are unlikely to know for sure who constructed them or when. Excavations are always expensive and destructive. The likelihood is therefore that a lot more research, including more detailed land surveys, would precede any digging, and that in any case these supposed barrows would compete against the other claims on archaeological funding.

Descend to Ham Gate and then follow the path running about 40m in from the wall in a southerly (Kingston Gate) direction. Cross the first culvert with wooden rails, and veer off on the small right hand path. Cross another drainage ditch which exits through a grating in the park wall, and shortly thereafter, where the path almost touches the park wall, you find yourself crossing a dip and a bank (8m wide x 0.5m high) that runs out from the park wall at a right angle.

In his *Monumenta Britannica*, John Aubrey, the great seventeenth century antiquarian, noted that

'In Ham-heath runs a straight Rampire from the [Richmond] Parke towards the Thames, having the graffe [trench] westwards: it is likely this was made as an obstacle to the Romans; I find several such in the west of England....'

It has never been formally identified but in his 1992 survey, Tom Greeves speculates that this may indeed be the end of Aubrey's 'Rampire' (4). One can see there is a 'graffe' on its west side and the bank seems to be the beginning of a more dramatic dyke now forming a path which runs across Ham Common almost parallel with Church Rd (and may be joined opposite the entrance to Wilmer House, where maintenance of the path may have modified it). It probably belongs to the late Iron Age (150BC - AD43) when iron tipped ploughs made the richer but heavier clay soils manageable for the first time, and so brought human settlements down off the gravel plateaux. Perhaps it is the delineation of a field system, or possibly an access causeway to the Thames across marshy ground, since fish would have been a major food source for any settlement near the river.

Resume the main path (about 75m in from the wall) towards Kingston Gate. When the path rises over a shoulder of higher ground you should see on top of the escarpment the unmistakable silhouette of a clump of pine trees above the deciduous trees. This is King's Clump ((5) on the map on p.37). Make for it. It stands almost directly above Gallows Pond. (This mid-nineteenth century pond is named after 'Gallows', the coppice that formed part of Kingston Common in the seventeenth century (Walk No. 3), which itself was named after the gallows that stood just outside the park wall).

King's Clump seems to be a well-defined barrow. It is noteworthy that all these probable barrows, with the exception of Oliver's Mound, are sited on the very edge of the Thames valley escarpment, commanding the view across the valley. It is difficult to escape the conclusion that siting was an important feature of barrow construction.

Proceed in a north easterly direction, parallel to the carriageway in the direction of Robin Hood Gate, passing Ladderstile Gate on your right and making for the car park at the top of Broomfield Hill (1.5km). Pass through the car park and begin walking down Broomfield Hill following a footpath that leads straight down the hill as the carriageway curves to the left. As it descends, the path crosses the remains of two or three concentric banks (6) that more or less follow the curve of

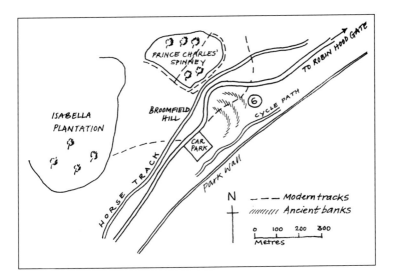

the hill around the edge of Broomfield Hill Wood.

Greeves thinks it is possible that these banks were defensive in purpose. Broomfield Hill lies just over a mile away from the more impressive fort at Caesar's Camp on Wimbledon Common. Hill forts became common during the Iron Age, from 500BC until 150BC when their construction declined. Incidentally, Aubrey remarked on Caesar's Camp: 'It is certain that this fortification was built by the Danes...methinks they are too artish for the old Britons.' What does the fellow mean, too *artish*?

The quickest way back to Pembroke Lodge is to skirt the north east side of Isabella plantation and cross Pond Slade, making for White Ash Lodge, Oak Lodge and thence to Pembroke Lodge (2.5km). (At the outset of this journey you may care to explore the cutting through Prince Charles' Spinney which is strewn with daffodils in spring.)

AFTERWORD

Another suspected and possibly important prehistoric site, identified by Greeves, lies in the southern part of Sidmouth Wood and is inaccessible to the public. Two parallel banks, about 40m apart, with ditches on the outside, extend for just over 300m. He speculates that these might be part of a *cursus*, a ritual structure of the third millennium BC. One reason for his thinking that they are probably prehistoric in age is that there is no evidence of any agricultural activity in this part of the park, then part of Petersham Common, before its enclosure in 1637.

The Park in the late Middle Ages

The medieval traces in the park are subtle, difficult to spot, but highly rewarding if you try to imagine the landscape as it might have been, even though we have few clues regarding what happened to it during the middle ages.

The settlements of Ham, Petersham and Kingston all probably date back to the seventh century AD, and possibly earlier. In 1086 William the Conqueror's *Domesday Book* was completed. It catalogued human settlements, landholders, size of cultivable lands, woodlands, pasturage and meadows, the population and productive potential. The areas around the park were among the more populous in Surrey, but with perhaps 15 persons per square mile it remained astonishingly sparse compared with today.

The manor of Kingston stretched to Kew, and included the lands of the manor of Shene (known as Richmond from 1501). It had a population of probably about 300. The manor of Shene first appears as a separate entity in 1130. Petersham, held by Chertsey Abbey since the early tenth century, probably had a population of only 60 people. From the mid-thirteenth century Merton Priory, second only to Southwark among the religious foundations of Surrey, held Hartington Combe, a twelfth century manor on the Ham/Mortlake manorial border, now the area around White Lodge Hill/Spanker's Hill and the Pen Ponds car park. But almost half of what became the park was in the manor of Mortlake, held by the archbishops of Canterbury.

Until the population grew it is unlikely that the poor soils of the park were used much except as rough pasture and coppiced woods. In prehistoric times the wooden plough was not strong enough to turn the richer clay soils in the valley. Thus people had preferred to live on the poorer upland soils. With the invention of the iron-tipped plough and the employment of oxen, people abandoned the uplands for the Thames valley.

However, traces on the landscape indicate that cultivable areas within what became the park were indeed brought under the plough during the middle ages, probably in the period 1150-1250 when, as a result of population growth, the extent of village arable land doubled all over England as waste lands were reclaimed. Some of the major boundary banks and ditches that can still be found in the park were probably dug in this period.

Fortunately, a map was drawn by Nicholas Lane between 1632 and 1637 (see p.10) indicating what the park wall would enclose. While we do not know definitely how old the details on this map are, the probability is that many of the field boundaries and roads date well back into the middle ages. One reason for this assumption is that some oaks, approximately 500 years old, still survive in the park, some indicating old hedgerows, others marking parish or manorial boundaries. Although Lane's map contains inaccuracies, it still provides a fascinating insight into what preceded the park. Although Lane marks more fields in private tenure than was likely to have been the case in the late middle ages, he still shows the manorial common lands, one of Mortlake's open fields 'Upper Town Field', and marks coppices and hayfields, the former vital for wooden tools, the latter as the only winter feed for livestock.

There are three principal medieval features in the park: ridge and furrow ploughing; banks, ditches or ancient trees which are the vestiges of field hedgerows or boundaries; and roads. Two routes ran through the park, one from Mortlake to Ham (which entered the park at the west end of Teck Plantation (west of East Sheen Gate) and the other from Shene (Richmond Gate) to Coombe (Ladderstile Gate). They intersected at Ham Cross. There were also access roads to farmland, notably to Hartleton (as Hartington became known by the seventeenth century) farm.

2 *The north-eastern section of the park*

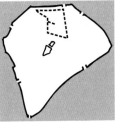

(5km/2 hours)

(On which one may see field boundaries, ridge and furrow ploughing and follow a section of the Mortlake-Ham road.)

ONLY UNDERTAKE THIS WALK BETWEEN MID-DECEMBER AND MAY WHEN GROUND COVER IS MINIMAL. SOME FEATURES ARE DIFFICULT TO SPOT. DO NOT SPOIL YOUR WALK HUNTING TOO LONG FOR THEM. YOU MAY NOTICE THEM ANOTHER TIME WHEN YOU WALK THAT WAY.

Start: Go to Bog Gate (closest car park at East Sheen Gate), and walk 100m to the SE corner of the metal fenced enclosure adjoining the park wall to the west of Bog Gate.

This is the intersection of what are probably the western and northern boundaries (7) of Hill Farm, see map on p.29. The western boundary of Hill Farm is the distinct ditch and bank following the line of an unsurfaced path (parallel and 50m west of the gravel path leading from Bog Gate).

Follow it and cross the horse ride and continue to follow it till it peters out. Another 60 paces brings you to a line of ancient oaks (8) and a slight ditch, running NW-SE towards Holly (Bog) Lodge.

These oaks are medieval, 600 and possibly 700 years old, and were once part of a hedgerow. The oak at the NW end of the line possibly marks another field boundary (9) which then ran due south to an ancient oak close to the small pond on the east side of Conduit Wood.

Return towards the intersection of the northern and western boundaries of Hill Farm, and go to the north east corner of the Riding Ring.

From here you may see that you are close to the edge of a slight bank (50 paces north) running from the corner of the metal fencing enclosure roughly SE towards the northern edge of Barn Wood. This is the northern boundary of Hill Farm, and presumably the track running along the northern edge of the farm marked on Lane's map (p.10). Hill Farm house ((10), illustrated on p.49) stood near the edge of the bank, but it is unclear whether it was standing there in the middle ages.

Follow the line of the bank (Hill Farm track) to the northern edge of Barn Wood.

If you consult Lane's map you will see that this is where Hill Fields adjoin Deane's Lane (11 and 12). Deane's Lane was an integral part of the road from Mortlake to Ham, an area surveyed in 1992. [If you wish to trace the Highway back to the edge of the park, it ran north-south from the kink in the western edge of Teck Plantation to about 20 metres west of the north west corner of the fencing of Two Storm Wood. On Lane's map the highway ran along the border between Little Heathe and Longe Lande.]

According to Greeves, a wooden building stood at this intersection, at the indent of the Two Storm Wood metal fencing close to the NW gate (currently locked), see map on p.31. It must have been a rudimentary, timber-framed structure with walls of thin wattle (interlaced coppiced wood, or tree shoots) and daub (dung and straw), its roof made of turf or thatch. The floor would have been earth, strewn with rushes. Stone or brick floors only came to be used by the peasantry in the late middle ages. The

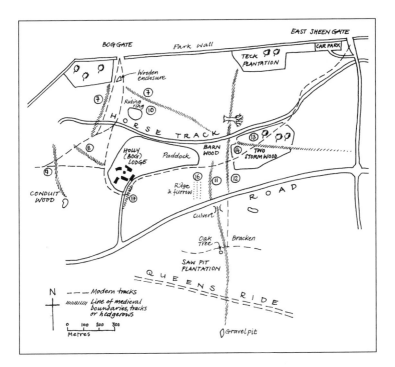

timber base would have eventually rotted in the ground and it had probably collapsed by Lane's time.

Later buildings had padstones or a stone or brick course to keep the wooden base off the ground. Wattle and daub was a very effective building material, so long as the timber frame was strong. However, it was progressively displaced in the seventeenth century by brick or stone, and rather unfairly dismissed, in the words of one contemporary, as little more than 'paper work'.

This building stood at the crossroads between Deane's Lane, the track from Hill Farm, and a 'warple way' (13), an agricultural access road, running west-east across Two Storm Wood.

Enter Two Storm Wood by the west gate.

The warple way is slightly sunken in Two Storm Wood, each end marked by a metal gate (on NW and E sides), and is a causeway across the open ground to the east (to the East Sheen carriageway). [It is very difficult to discern, except from Sheen Cross from where the long low line of the causeway is plainly visible]. On Lane's map the warple way divided Longe Lande and Bittin Furlongs in the Mortlake Upper Town Field. The Hill Farm-warple way track was still in use in the mid-eighteenth century, as can be seen on Eyre's map (p.55).

Note Deane's Coppice (14) on Lane's Map, lying south of the warple way in Two Storm Wood. Coppiced wood, hazel, hornbeam, field maple or alder, was an essential feature of any village in the middle ages, to provide the basic material for wattle (for infilling timber frame buildings and for fencing) and all manner of wooden implements. By the late fourteenth century coppicing was highly developed, with the nurturing of trees of the same species but varied ages in order to ensure a constant and standard production of wood. Coppices were harvested every 6 to 12 years, and usually enclosed to protect them from livestock. Deane's coppice contains a number of ancient timber yielding oaks, sometimes planted to provide timber as well as the 'underwood' of the coppice. It is currently planned to replant this coppice.

The west side of Deane's Coppice is lined by the metal fence. A large oak about 60 paces south east of the NW Gate marks the north east corner of the coppice. A slight bank runs down the east side of the coppice (15), most easily discernible looking back from the carriageway.

Return to the west gate of Two Storm Wood.

Deane's Lane still has two quite distinct 'hollow ways' or sunken lanes running almost parallel through Barn Wood.

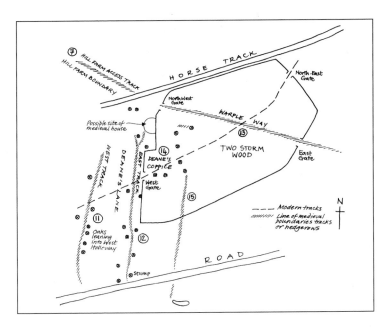

The western track of Deane's Lane (11) is the easier to follow. It lies 75 paces or so west of the west edge of Two Storm Wood.

It is most easily observable at the southern end, close to the Richmond-Roehampton carriageway where the ground is boggy and the oaks tend to lean inwards, from the old banks into the sunken lane.

Before proceeding towards Ham along the holloway, the south west part of Barn Wood (west of Deane's Lane) is a good area for observing ridge and furrow ploughing running north-south. Ridge and furrow is a subtle feature and difficult to spot. You may have to get close to the ground to see the 'ripple' of the furrows, or walk slowly westwards, parallel to the carriage way, to the west edge of Barn Wood and you should notice you are crossing regular undulations.

A brief background to ridge and furrow may be helpful. The Saxons introduced an 'open field' system of farming. Although there were many local variations, one may generalise as follows. Within the village each household might be expected to hold a 'croft', probably about seven acres. Beyond the village lay the open fields, usually three of them, and perhaps about 100 acres each in size. These fields were held communally. Each field would usually follow an annual cycle to produce a winter crop, for example wheat or rye, in the first year and a spring crop, barley or oats, in the second. In the third year it lay fallow and livestock grazed on it. Each farmer would be assigned strips in each field.

Because a yoke of up to eight oxen was difficult to turn it made sense to farm one long furrow. For this reason large open fields were divided into strips between the village farmers. In theory each strip was one 'furrow long' or furlong (220 yards) in length, but there were inevitably variations. The width between furrows varies from one era to another. The wider they are, the older they are likely to be. The widest (12m) and probably oldest (possibly Saxon, and in the gift of Chertsey Abbey) are on low ground beside Ham Gate. The furrows in Barn Wood are approximately 9m wide. Later, yet narrower furrows reflect improved ploughing technology which required fewer oxen.

This particular strip farming was abandoned in, or after, the fourteenth century and planted with oaks and is identified on Lane's Map as 'Hill Coppice' (16). Why was the old field abandoned? We may only speculate. During the late thirteenth and early fourteenth centuries the English economy expanded rapidly, with increasing demand for timber and fuel. We know for example that the Abbot of Chertsey, 1307-46, who held Petersham manor, was assiduous in thickening and planting woods. However, there is also another possible reason. In 1348-9, the Black Death killed over one third of the population, and land all over Europe went out of production. This, too, might have occasioned the replacement of cultivated land with woods which demanded little labour, and also afforded feed in the form of acorns for swine.

Beyond the open fields system lay the common pasturage, usually the poorest waste ground on which manorial tenants could graze livestock, or gather wood, rushes or turf.

Across the greensward beyond Barn Wood, the approach road to Holly (Bog) Lodge crosses the western edge of Adder Downe (17), marked on Lane's Map. It is readily visible, marked by a slight bank and a row of oak trees. It is marked on the sketch map for this walk and you may care to note it when you next pass that way.

For the doggedly curious: the eastern track (12) is harder to identify but runs parallel to and about 15m west of the west edge of Two Storm Wood fence, down to the Richmond-Roehampton carriageway where the ground is usually boggy and you can see that the oaks lean inwards from the old banks to the sunken lane. This part of Deane's Lane is lost on the far side of the carriageway.
Return to the bottom end of Deane's Lane (West).

The western track of Deane's Lane/Mortlake-Ham road (11) can be followed across the carriageway where it is built up as a causeway, presumably over what was boggy ground.

Find the (almost buried) brick culvert under the causeway, about 30 paces from the carriageway. After another 15 paces, note an old oak tree on your left, and you will observe it stands on a low bank running to Barn Wood Pond.

This is probably the southern boundary of Deane's Coppice.

Continue walking up the causeway, running well nigh straight up the hill to Saw Pit Plantation more or less along the line of the path entering the bracken towards the top of the hill, slightly on the left of the path. Enter Saw Pit Plantation on the path, and about fifteen paces to your left you should locate the holloway,

a very slight trough in the ground, running almost parallel with the path. It is quite difficult to locate, but it remains quite close to, and left of, the path across the plantation to Queen's Ride, although it is obstructed by one or two fallen trees. If you find parts of it, your faith will be vindicated when you cross the Queen's Ride where the remains of the holloway is visible as a ripple in the Ride. The holloway is finally lost in the flooded gravel pit the far side of the Queen's Ride.

Walk down the Queen's Ride to the White Lodge.

Here you can locate perhaps the most obvious example of ridge and furrow in the whole park, on the triangle of ground surrounded by tarmac carriageways just south of the White Lodge, the furrows running east-west. Other good examples may be found north of the White Lodge or in Duchess Wood north west of the White Lodge, in both cases the furrows running west-east. In these two cases cultivation was abandoned and the land wooded.

Return to East Sheen Gate following the road from the White Lodge (1.3km).

Lane's map indicates that the tarmac carriageway approximately overlays a road which served Hartleton Farm (as Hartington manor became known by the seventeenth century).

3 *The South West Section of the Park*

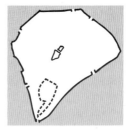

(3km/1 hour)

DO NOT ATTEMPT THIS WALK EXCEPT BETWEEN
MID-DECEMBER AND MAY WHEN GROUND COVER IS MINIMAL. SOME
FEATURES ARE DIFFICULT TO SPOT.

The final and most impressive section of the Shene (Richmond)-Coombe road (18) merits a visit on its own, see map on p.37. It will be recalled from the introduction to the park in the late middle ages, that this highway crossed the Mortlake-Ham road at Ham Cross, and runs up to Dann's Pond, and is quite distinctly marked on Lane's map (p.10), with Lambert Hawe on its western side and Nine Acres, Sixteen Acres and Blacke Heathe on its eastern side.

Start: Park in the car park at Kingston Gate. Cross the road. Ahead you will see a track running across the greensward towards Gallows Pond. However, turn right and follow the path running uphill into the trees close to the road up Kingston Hill. Stop at the tree line and find the bank running northwards more or less along the tree line (19).

This has been identified by Greeves as the western boundary of 'Gallows', clearly marked on Lane's map. ('Gallows' is probably a reference to the gallows that stood just outside the present Kingston Gate.) If you follow this bank, you may notice a kink in it, the beginning of a ditch running off to the left (westwards). This would appear to be the boundary between Little Common Field and Hare Snatch on Lane's map.

Continue along the boundary bank of Gallows.

It brings you down to Gallows Pond, through the Canadian Sugar Maple plantation, roughly where the northern edge of Hare Snatch seems to have been.

Follow the path past Gallows Pond.

The beginning of the 'bulge' marked on Lane's map as Mr Price's border with Gallows seems to run out from the pond across your path and into the trees, but it is difficult to follow.

Proceed up the path to Thatched House Lodge. When you reach the tarmac you will see two informal paths running in a northerly direction. Take the right hand path that runs to the left of Coronation Plantation. After 50m you reach a large oak tree on your left and four others on your right. Follow the slight ditch running off to the left for 30 paces to the rotting remains of a tree, which lies at the head of a depression. Follow the depression running parallel with the path you have just left.

This is a medieval field boundary(20). It clearly predates Lane since it runs straight across Lambert Hawe.

Just before the boundary ditch plunges into the stream note on your left broken ground with a circular earthwork (21).

Greeves believes this was some kind of medieval enclosure, possibly for livestock.

Cross the stream and follow the path up the far side. Just before you reach the junction with another footpath and the horsetrack, note the depression in the bracken on your right. This is the Shene-Coombe highway (18). Follow it for 120 paces. Then climb up to the horse track and you should see a

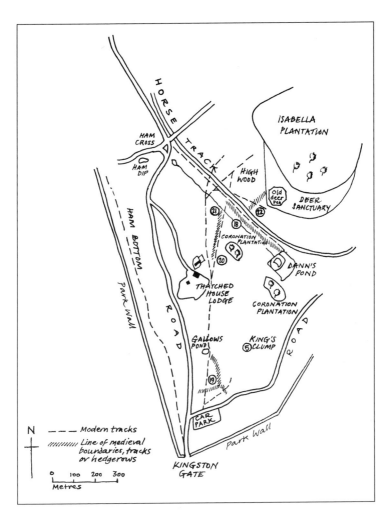

**bank and ditch (22) running at a right angle into High Wood.
Follow this bank to the old deer pen on the edge of the deer
sanctuary in High Wood.**

This bank marks the boundary hedgerow between Sixteen Acres
and Blacke Heathe, both on Lane's map. Incidentally, some of the
pollarded oaks to be found on the Blacke Heathe (now part of High

Wood) are probably 600 years old and may be aboriginal woodland. Rare beetles, also found in Savernake forest, Wiltshire, one of southern England's only surviving ancient woodlands, have been identified here.

Return to, and continue up the Shene-Coombe highway to Dann's Pond (enclosed by fencing and trees), where it peters out. Proceed around Dann's Pond in a clockwise direction and return to Kingston Gate car park.

AFTERWORD

One other major medieval feature should be noted. Although Beverley Brook, which runs across the eastern side of the park, has been straightened and embanked in recent times, its name testifies to its early medieval origins: 'Beaver stream' ('ley' is the corrupted form of *lacu*: Anglo Saxon for stream). Beavers became extinct in England in the eleventh or twelfth century and the name presumably predates this.

The Enclosure of Richmond Park in the Seventeenth Century

Richmond Park is a misnomer. Until its enclosure in 1637 the park comprised lands belonging mainly to Ham (895 acres), Mortlake (732 acres), Petersham (306 acres) and Roehampton (200 acres). Kingston, Richmond and Putney lands constituted 117, 69 and 36 acres respectively. The park got its name through its association with the royal palace of Richmond.

The fact is that the gravelly uplands made poor arable land but good hunting country, and Charles I began to covet it for his own pleasure. In the words of a contemporary, Edward Hyde Earl of Clarendon, who set it down in his *History of the Rebellion and the Civil Wars of England:*

'The King [Charles I], who was excessively affected to Hunting, and the Sports of the Field, had a great desire to make a great Park for Red, as well as Fallow Deer, between Richmond and Hampton Court where he had large Wasts of his own and great parcels of Wood....'

He wanted something larger than the hunting parks of his predecessors, notably the 370 acre park beside the river created by his father, James I. Yet, as Clarendon pointed out,

'...some Parishes had Commons in those Wasts, so, many Gentlemen, and Farmers, had good Houses, and good Farms intermingled with those Wasts of their own Inheritance, or for their Lives, or Years; and without taking of Them into the Park, it would not be of the largeness, or for the use proposed.'

Lane's map (p.10), probably surveyed in 1632 (or even earlier) but finalised in January 1637, shows how many landholders the King had to deal with. Basically four kinds of lands were involved, privately held lands, demesne (or manorial) lands that were leased out, manorial open fields and common pasturage. Some holdings were extensive, for example Henry White's Hill Farm in the north-west part of Mortlake; Humfry Bennet's plots in both Roehampton and Mortlake; above all, Gregory Cole's substantial holdings in the manors of Ham and Petersham and also Hartleton Farm, originally a separate manor belonging to Merton Priory.

Charles anticipated no difficulty in persuading the private and manorial land holders involved to surrender their respective lands if he offered generous terms. In December 1634 he began negotiations to purchase the properties in his proposed 'New Park'. His intentions soon made him unpopular, not merely in those parishes affected, but also in the City of London where his high-handed behaviour was already resented. Both the Lord Treasurer and the Chancellor of the Exchequer vainly sought to dissuade him from making himself so needlessly unpopular.

The following April, when he had barely secured five acres, he ordered the construction of a nine foot high wall around the whole area he coveted, the bricks being made on site. It was completed in less than three years, but there was difficulty in assembling a sufficient local workforce probably because the whole enterprise was so unpopular. At any rate instructions were issued early in 1636 to 'all Mayors and others the King's officers' to assist him 'in taking up the required bricklayers, labourers, carts and carriages.' But the wall was built too hastily and had to be extensively repaired over the next 25 years. The wall still requires constant maintenance, and is probably in a better state today than it has ever been in the past.

With the wall being built before their very eyes, most land holders reluctantly came to terms, accepting the king's compulsory generosity with as good a grace as could be mustered. Those who refused to treat lost their land anyway.

4 *The Seventeenth Century Walk*

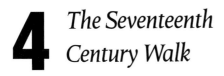

(6.5 km/1.5 hours)

The sketches of the houses once standing in the park are based upon indistinct depictions on the original map by Nicholas Lane and research into Surrey buildings of the late medieval to early Jacobean periods.

Start at the Pen Ponds car park. Find the bank (23) on the map on p.42, marking the boundary of 'Rutnells'.

One of those tenanted holdings to disappear with the enclosure, clearly marked on Lane's map, was Rutnells, a separate part of Hartleton Farm. Rutnells was an estate with two buildings, probably a cottage and a barn or stable. The shape and extent of Rutnells can be imagined from Lane's map (p.10), running from the present car park down almost to the Upper Pen Pond. It can be partly followed on the ground with the help of the sketch map, for those interested. How it acquired its name is a mystery, since there was no owner of this name.

Take the road to Ham Cross, but after 200m turn half left onto a broad grassy footpath, just before two standard trees on the left of the carriageway. After 20 paces note a ditch running in at right angles from your left. This is the northern boundary of Wheate Fieldes, marked on Lane's map. Having crossed your path it turns to follow the line of the path in the form of a very slight bank on its right side. In many places this western boundary of Wheate Fieldes (24) is barely detectable, even when the summer growth has died back, but becomes clearer

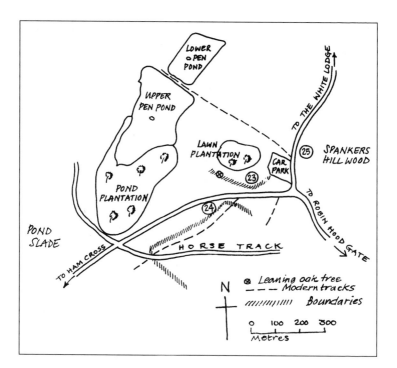

again as you approach the horse track (400m). Stop immediately you have crossed the horse track to note a ditch running off at a right angle to your left.

Wheate Fieldes/Ox Pasture is clearly marked on Lane's map. You are now standing at the southwestern corner of the field. It forms part of one of the major holdings of Gregory Cole, which included The Great Sleyt, Gibbet Close and The Sleyt, thus covering an area including most of the present Isabella Plantation up to the park wall approximately from Broomfield Hill to Ladderstile Gate.

Follow the horse track (i.e turn right) back to the carriageway and walk to Ham Cross.

On your right you will pass Pond Plantation and Pond Slade (a 'slade' is an open greensward or expanse of boggy ground), and will already have passed the Upper Pen Pond.

In 1636 Edward Manning, who was already building the park wall, was commissioned to carry out 'railing in copses, the making of a pond, the cutting of lawns, etc, in the New Park at Richmond, and for bringing a river to run through the same.' Since Beverley Brook had already long been in existence, the river in question was probably that marked on Lane's map, to drain water from the slade through what became the two Pen Ponds and finally into Beverley Brook.

It is also likely that Manning's new pond was the embryo Upper Pen Pond. In 1650 we know that a punt was in use on 'the pond' and that between 1673-83 over 8,000 loads (presumably cartloads) of gravel were removed from the park for use in the local building industry. There are several gravel pits in the park, some now ponds. The Lower Pen Pond, if not the Upper, was probably the main gravel pit. Even once the Pen Ponds had been dug to their present extent, possibly at the very end of the century, they were still known as 'The Canals'. The original 'Pen Pond', now known as Leg of Mutton Pond, lies 200m west of the Pen Ponds. It probably acquired its name from the proximity of a deer pen. Alas, it seems to have nothing to do with the more romantic but ill-founded theory that these ponds were intentionally for 'pens', the word used for female swans in the sixteenth century.

Continue across Ham Cross, and walk 150m past the small pond in Ham Dip.

This is the site of Loanes House (26) in Ham that had belonged to a William Clifton. He had died in 1633 and his executor had promptly leased the buildings, three of which fell within the proposed park as shown by Lane, along with 28 acres for a period of 21 years. Now he had to negotiate the cancellation of the lease,

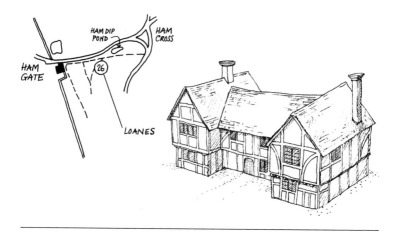

and in 1637 surrendered this land for the park, presumably
providing the new lessee with a portion of the royal compensation.

The original version of Lane's map includes a crude sketch of
Loanes. Lane's depiction seems to be a two-storey timber framed
building, infilled with brick or wattle and daub, and double gabled,
possibly with two chimney stacks. These features are indicative of
the major progress made in housing in the period 1450-1600. A
brick chimney and also either brick or stone base that took the
timber house off the wet earth had been affordable only by
wealthier country people in the middle ages. Chimney technology
ensured both a hotter fire and smoke free rooms, while stone or tile
floors substantially reduced the level of damp. By 1600 these two
features had become commonplace for virtually everyone. Within
the year all three buildings had been demolished, and the name
'Loanes' transferred to the one surviving building that stood where
the present Park Gate House stands, outside Ham Gate.

Turn right and walk along Ham Bottom to Petersham Gate (1.75km).

Here stood one of the principal properties inside the proposed

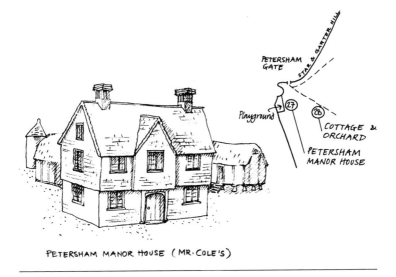

PETERSHAM MANOR HOUSE (MR. COLE'S)

enclosure, Petersham manor house (27), occupied on leasehold from Charles I's wife Henrietta Maria by Gregory Cole. Cole's holding was described as 'a whole tenement and a dovecote, barn, stables, etc.'. Lane depicts the main building as of contemporary design, having two chimney stacks.

In fact Cole held almost 800 acres in four separate areas of what became the park. We have already passed Rutnells and Wheate Fields (up to Ladderstile Gate) which, together with the third area on Spanker's Hill-White Lodge Hill, comprised Hartleton Farm. His Petersham holding included the adjacent lands marked Rex Berrygrove and Rex The Warren.

It must have been Cole of whom Clarendon wrote 'a Gentleman, who had the best Estate, with a convenient House and Gardens, would by no means part with it.' However, in the end he disconsolately surrendered his lands, made over his remaining leaseholds in Ham and Petersham to William Murray (soon to be Earl of Dysart and the new occupant of Ham House), and left Petersham for good. One may imagine his *schadenfreude* when

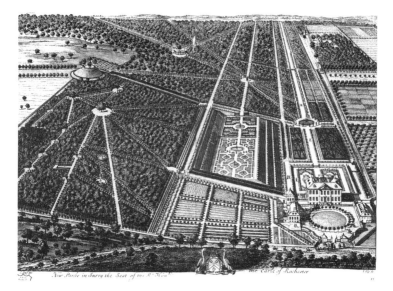

'New Park' seat of the Earl of Rochester (engraving by I. Kip, 1708 from a drawing by Leonard Kuyff). Note King Henry VIII's mound and the avenue to its left.

Petersham Park, built in 1732 to a design by Lord Burlington.

King Charles began to come unstuck politically a couple of years later.

Petersham Lodge, as the manor house now became known, was not demolished but became accommodation for one of the first two deputy park keepers, Ludovic Carlile, and subsequently for Sir Lionel Tollemache who became joint keeper with his wife Elizabeth, Lord Dysart's daughter. Tollemache and the Countess of Dysart, as Elizabeth now became, moved into Ham House on the death of her father. Elizabeth, in the words of a contemporary,

'.... was a woman of great beauty, but of far greater parts; had a wonderful quickness of apprehension, and an amazing vivacity in conversation.....but what ruined these accomplishments, she was restless in her ambition, profuse in her expense, and of a ravenous covetousness; nor was there anything she stuck at to compass her end, for she was violent in everything – a violent friend and a much more violent enemy.'

She thus saw off Sir Daniel Harvey, Lord of Coombe Neville on the south side of the park, who had sought the Rangership following the Restoration in 1660. Against so ruthlessly formidable a person he did not stand a chance. Then she seems to have turned her fell attention on the two deputy keepers. Humfry Rogers abandoned his post in 1661, and Carlile two years later. When she was widowed in 1669 she married the Duke of Lauderdale, himself notoriously brutal. They must have made a terrifying couple. When he died in 1683 Elizabeth surrendered the Park Keepership and also Petersham Lodge both of which passed to Lawrence Hyde, Earl of Rochester. Hyde was a son of Clarendon and brother-in-law to James Duke of York (later James II). In 1686 Hyde obtained a personal lease of over 50 acres including the old Petersham Lodge which he promptly demolished and replaced with a magnificent mansion, 'New Park'. It did not last very long. In 1721 a fire destroyed it. The land was sold, and in the 1730s the Earl of Harrington commissioned Lord Burlington, the great Palladian exponent of his day, to build a new lodge. The new 'Petersham Park' remained formally separated from the rest of Richmond Park until 1833 (see Walk No. 7).

Walk up the hill following the wall to Richmond Gate (1km).

A small private property, marked on Lane's map, a cottage and orchard (28) stood on the slopes of Petersham Park, about half way between Petersham Gate and Pembroke Lodge. This was presumably demolished after its surrender in 1637.

From Richmond Gate strike across country to Conduit Wood (0.5km).

As marked on Lane's map you will find here the 'White Conduit', a brick-capped spring, more imaginatively christened 'the Bomb Shelter' by local children. The White Conduit was one of three channels presumably constructed in about 1500 (but it may be older) to supply water to the new Palace of Shene (Richmond) on the Green. (The other two

The White Conduit
(a) as it appears on Lane's map
(b) the shape suggested by
surviving Tudor brickwork

were Red Conduit which lay on Richmond Hill, probably in the area of Onslow Road, and a riverside conduit probably close to Bridge St.) The original Tudor brick part is within the south western end of the current structure. It is difficult to know exactly what it may have looked like. Its name, distinguishing it from the 'Red Conduit', may arise from a white mortar rendering applied to the exterior brickwork. It was still in use when much of the Palace was dismantled during the Commonwealth, 1649-60.

During repairs to the structure in January 1996 a Victorian brass valve was unearthed. John Cloake, with his encyclopaedic local knowledge, has speculated that this may well have been installed by Joseph Ellis, proprietor of the Star and Garter Hotel (where the Star and Garter Home now stands) from 1822 onwards. For Ellis '.... found a pure spring and a perpetual one in Richmond Park and conducted the same to his own house [the Star and Garter] for general service as drinking water.'

Walk across to the edge of Holly (Bog) Lodge, turn left and follow perimeter around to the Riding Ring above it (0.75km).

Just on the north east side of the Riding Ring stood the two buildings of Henry White's Hill Farm (10), visible on Lane's map (see also Walk No 2, p.28), still just

HILL FARM

discernable by broken ground. White lived more modestly than either Clifton or Cole. Lane depicts his farmhouse with a central chimney, and with another building, presumably a barn. However, his landholdings were still substantial: primarily 56 acres on Hill Farm itself, another 12 acres of arable in the Mortlake common field, 30 acres of copse named Slawood, and also part of Beverley Close which he let to a Mr Offley.

Return to the Pen Ponds car park (2km) – the most direct route is: continue following the perimeter of Bog Lodge. When it turns right, go half right through Barn Wood, cross the carriageway

and, passing Barn Wood Pond, turn up the valley running south to the Pen Ponds, cross the causeway between the two ponds and continue to the car park.

HARTLETON FARM

Lane shows three buildings at Hartleton. The main farmhouse (25) stood at the foot of Spankers Hill, close to the car park, and, Lane suggests, boasted two chimney stacks and a gable end. It was probably built before tiles began to replace thatch, and is therefore unlikely to be later than 1550. A second building apparently had one chimney. The farm had belonged to Gregory's father, George, since 1605.

It will be recalled that Rutnells and also the Wheate Fieldes up to Gibbet Close (separated from the rest of Hartleton by Beverley Plain) were also parts of this farm. The third section, in which the farmhouse lay, included Hill, Home, Middle and Bottom Closes, Broade Fielde, Beverley Close, and Priors Hill Copse (on Beverley Close and Priors Hill Copse, see p.104).

Charles allocated Hartleton Farm to his other deputy park

keeper, Humfry Rogers. Hartleton Farm was delapidated, lacking the style and comfort of Petersham manor house, and Rogers promptly rebuilt it. In due course it became the residence of the Keeper, after the separation of Petersham Park. In the early eighteenth century, when it acquired the name 'the Old Lodge', it was enlarged by Lord Walpole, who was Keeper at the time (see Walk No. 5).

AFTERWORD

Following the execution of Charles I, Parliament vested the Corporation of the City of London in July 1649 with custodianship of the park, 'excepting timber trees', i.e. those large enough to provide oak timbers for the navy. With a nose for a quick profit, the Corporation immediately started felling other saleable timber. Alarmed by this rampant asset-stripping, Parliament passed a Resolution the following February

> 'That the Parliament doth declare, that it was the Intention of the Parliament in passing the Act for settling the new Park at Richmond on the Mayor and Commonalty of the City of London, that the same should be preserved as a Park still, without Destruction; and to remain as an Ornament to the City, and a Mark of Favour from the Parliament unto the said City.'

In 1660 the Corporation moved swiftly to mend its fences with the restored monarchy. It handed the park to Charles II within four days of his return to London.

Some sixty years later George I urgently needed £2,000 and proposed selling park timber. His Surveyor-General, possibly mindful of Parliament's previous ruling, sternly reminded him 'the wood in Richmond Park is rather for ornament than profit.'

The Park in the Eighteenth Century

In 1727 George II appointed Robert, Lord Walpole, as Ranger,
though it was his father, Sir Robert Walpole, the Prime Minister,
who exercised effective superintendence and enjoyed the benefit.
Sir Robert was already a passionate hunter in the park and for the
next quarter century the park was regularly used for this purpose.
Another avid hunter was that most zestful of women, Lady Mary
Wortley Montagu, best known for her wonderful Turkish letters,
who at the age of 35 wrote to her sister:

> 'I pass many hours on horseback, and I'll assure you, ride stag
> hunting, which I know you'll stare to hear of. I have arrived to
> vast courage and skill that way, and am so well pleased with it
> as with the acquisition of a new sense. His Royal Highness
> [later George II] hunts in Richmond Park, and I make one of the
> *beau monde* of his train. I desire you after this account not to
> name the word old woman to me any more. I approach to fifteen
> nearer than I did ten years ago, and am in hopes to improve
> every year in health and vivacity.'

Sir Robert Walpole himself was so devoted to the chase that he
retired to the Old Lodge (old Hartleton Farm) which he had
extensively remodelled, for Saturdays as well as Sundays,
instructing the Commons to abandon its previous habit of sitting
on Saturdays. It is thus that we arguably owe the two-day week-end
to hunting in Richmond Park. Sir Robert died in 1745, his son six
years later in 1751. In the early nineteenth century the Old Lodge
fell into disrepair and was demolished in 1841.

It should not be thought that sport was confined to deer
hunting. There were wild turkey too. Turkey had been introduced to
Britain in 1521, and into the park in about 1690. In the early
eighteenth century there were probably over 3,000 turkeys in the

park, living off the then abundant supply of acorns. Dogs were used to flush them from the ground cover – there was extensive gorse in the park until the twentieth century – up into the trees where they could be shot.

Virtually all the old oak trees in the park have been pollarded (the branches removed, allowing fresh growth around the central trunk). Pollarding has several purposes. It ensures a supply of timber, with timber-bearing trees usually being pollarded every seven years. It also ensures healthier and longer-living trees, since allowing large branches to die and fall off renders trees more liable to rot. However, pollarding in the eighteenth century may also have been in order to ensure that these wild turkeys settled in lower branches where they could more easily be bagged. There is nothing quite like the British sense of fair play when it comes to field sports. [Another theory regarding pollarding in the park is that it was to provide browse for the deer.] Edward Jesse, writing in 1834, has this to say:

'One of the keepers in Richmond Park informs me that he has often heard his father, who was also a keeper, mention that, in the reign of George the second, a large flock of wild turkies, consisting of not less than three thousand, was regularly kept up as part of the stock of the park..... They were hunted with dogs, and made to take refuge in a tree where they were frequently shot by George the second. I have not been able to learn how long they had been preserved in the park before his reign, but they were totally destroyed towards the latter end of it, in consequence of the dangers to which the keepers were exposed in protecting them from poachers, with whom they had many bloody fights, being frequently overpowered by them.'

The park more or less ceased to be a deer-hunting park after the Walpoles' demise and became more of a farm to provide venison for the royal and ministerial households. By the end of the century sport consisted of hare coursing, angling and partridge and

John Eyre's map of 1754

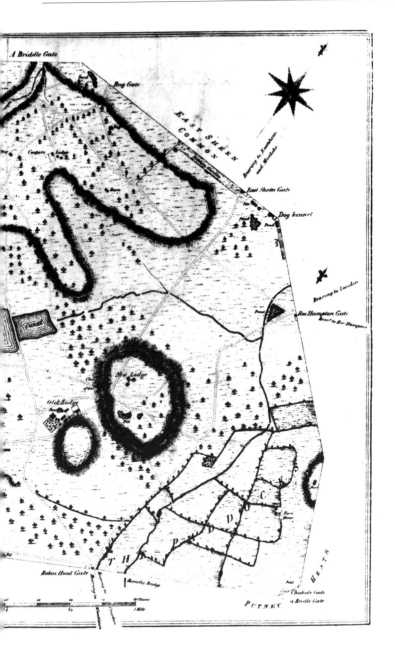

pheasant shooting. Partridges are still occasionally seen in the park.

Management of the park and its deer required the provision of housing for the various keepers and a number of houses appeared. These form the basis of Walk No. 5.

5 *The Eighteenth Century Buildings Walk*

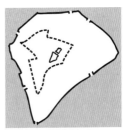

(8 km/2 hours)

Start: Pembroke Lodge car park.
Enter Pembroke Lodge gardens front entrance

Pembroke Lodge has humble origins. It was originally the Molecatcher's cottage, but during George II's reign was known as Hill Lodge and occupied by one of the park gamekeepers. However, towards the end of the century a court beauty, 'Eliza' Countess of Pembroke, persuaded George III (who had had sexual fantasies about her during his bouts of mental illness) to lease her the property. Sir John Soane remodelled and enlarged the property for her in the period 1785-95. By the time of her death in 1831, at the ripe old age of 94, Pembroke Lodge had acquired its present form, and acquired her name.

Pembroke Lodge was granted to Lord John Russell in 1847, one year after he had become Prime Minister. It remained in the Russell household until 1929. (For the Russells, see Walk No. 7 and for the Russell School, see Walk No. 9.)

Proceed around the northern side of Sidmouth Wood, crossing the Richmond-Roehampton carriageway, to Holly (Bog) Lodge (1km).

In spite of the extra buildings, the lodge, probably constructed in the mid-1730s, retains great charm. It seems always to have been the head keeper's lodge. It may be the enlargement of a building originally known as Cooper's Lodge, presumably lived in by

Holly (Bog) Lodge in the eighteenth century

Joseph Cooper and his son Alexander (buried in Petersham churchyard, 1735 and 1775 respectively). The Coopers may well have been head keepers in their day, but we do not know for sure. In 1771 it became known as Lucas' Lodge, and one may infer that this was when Alexander Cooper retired and John Lucas assumed the office of head keeper.

Lucas was almost certainly the son of a Lucas recruited from the Duke of Newcastle's estate at Claremont (Esher) at the beginning of the century, a man renowned for his prowess in tackling poachers with the quarter staff. John Lucas died in 1795 and, since his own son, John, was deemed too young, he was succeeded by his deputy, James Sawyer, who had joined the park staff only eight years earlier but whose family had been engaged in deer-keeping for generations. Thus, James Sawyer moved into the head keeper's lodge and the young John Lucas moved out to the deputy keeper's house, White Ash Lodge (see below). It was briefly known as Holly Lodge, but acquired the name of Bog Lodge, on account of the bog to its north, drained only in the mid-nineteenth century. It has recently been renamed Holly Lodge.

Walk back along the access road to Holly Lodge, cross the main carriageway and walk 200m beyond, until the Queen's Ride lies on your left.

The Queen's Ride is a magnificent avenue, probably cut through existing woodland to the White Lodge. It was the final part of the private road completed for Queen Caroline, George II's consort, who habitually travelled between Richmond Lodge in the Old Deer Park and this new hunting lodge that soon became her favourite residence. She entered the park from Kew at Queen's Gate (now Bog Gate) which had been specially cut through the wall for her.

Walk the Queen's Ride to the White Lodge (1.2km).

The White Lodge, first known as Stone Lodge (on account of its Portland stone facing) and then as New Lodge to differentiate it from Old (Hartleton) Lodge 500 metres away (discussed in Walk No. 4), was built in the Palladian style in 1727. It was designed by

The White Lodge as originally designed

Roger Morris in partnership with his patron, the Earl of Pembroke. (They built Marble Hill, much more of an architectural landmark, the following year. Their greatest success was to reduce Palladio's idea for a triumphal bridge to the size required for an ornamental bridge at Lord Pembroke's own seat at Wilton, Wilts.)

One might question the siting of the two great houses so close together but they commanded about the best views in the park. Proximity may also have reflected the intimate relations between the royal family and the prime minister. George I, who did not live to see the lodge completed, greatly enjoyed Walpole's company hunting. After his death Queen Caroline and Sir Robert Walpole became close political allies, 'the two ears' of George II. Princess Amelia lived here when appointed ranger, 1751-61 (see Walk No. 6).

When George III took over the rangership in 1792 he immediately took an interest in the park, initiating extensive but unsuccessful attempts to drain boggy areas, re-routing the Richmond-Roehampton carriageway to maximise the aesthetic pleasure from the landscape of the park (as any car driver should notice), and experimenting with new agricultural methods on what is now the golf course. Sickness forced his retirement as Ranger in 1814.

Sadly, the White Lodge quickly lost its architectural integrity as a hunting box. Princess Amelia commissioned the construction of two side pavilions. These were designed by Stephen Wright, erstwhile clerk to William Kent, and resemble the side pavilions of Horse Guards, one of Kent's better known works. These slightly compromised the original effect, but the single storey colonnades to the side pavilions minimised the visual impact of these extensions.

George III had used the White Lodge but never lived in it. In 1801 he insisted that his newly appointed prime minister, Henry Addington, should live at the White Lodge. Addington proved an unusually ineffectual prime minister and resigned in 1804, but was

Humphry Repton's landscape proposals: before.

able to stay on at the White Lodge. In 1813, as Viscount Sidmouth, he took over the management of the park as deputy-ranger (see Walk No. 7), something he was very much better at.

George III was anxious that the White Lodge, still really only a hunting pavilion, should be large enough for Addington and his family, and he commissioned James Wyatt, the Gothic revivalist, to convert the property into a country house. Wyatt already had a controversial reputation. His 'restorations' of medieval cathedrals had already earned him the epithet 'The Destroyer'. Now he was given a free hand and he duly spoilt the appearance of the White Lodge with two-storey corridors leading to modified flank pavilions.

Meanwhile, the first man to describe himself as a landscape gardener, Humphry Repton (1752-1818), was set to work on the grounds in 1805. He had been a student of Lancelot 'Capability' Brown. Repton always prepared a 'Red Book', his manuscript proposals bound in red morocco. Like other contemporaries,

Humphry Repton's landscape proposals: after.

Repton usually favoured a vista of raw nature after the more contrived landscapes of the mid-eighteenth century. But the White Lodge was a good deal more public than a private park. Having considered ideas of a ha-ha (a ditch concealing a fence), which he considered too public, and of a belt of trees and shrubs, which he decided would prove too enclosed, he uncharacteristically opted for what he called 'the ancient formal style', commending 'the neatness and security of a gravel walk' to replace the 'uncleanly, pathless grass of a forest, filled with troublesome animals of every kind, and some occasionally dangerous'. His Red Book 'before' illustration, suggests the mayhem caused by deer and other livestock, not to mention casually abandoned hurdles, convincing evidence of how plucky we all are to stroll in such deer-infested pastures. Repton had his way, but he was hardly the man for Richmond Park and his skills were more happily employed in Russell Square and Kensington Gardens. Today the White Lodge sadly remains an architectural mess. While Repton's formal garden

The Old Lodge c. 1780

has disappeared, Wyatt's additions remain and the key view from the Queen's Ride is marred by the wooden fence.

Walk along the tarmac carriageway to the Pen Ponds car park.

The Old Lodge at the foot of Spanker's Hill remained the regular home of the Deputy Ranger until the early nineteenth century when it became little used, and then fell into disrepair and was finally demolished in 1841. What is remarkable is that virtually no surface traces remain, except for a circular depression probably marking the site of a well, up the slope just behind the house, and few bricks lying in the ground.

Take the carriageway to Ham Cross, but strike half left after 100m along a broad grassy path. Follow it, across the horse track, until you reach the Disabled car park on the edge of the Isabella Plantation. Continue straight across, crossing another

horse track down into the gully, crossing the brick culvert, and up the far side to Thatched House Lodge (2.5km).

Thatched House Lodge probably originated as a small building constructed for deer keepers in the 1670s. It seems to have been inhabited by a Charles Aldridge, buried in Petersham churchyard in 1736. It was about this time that Sir Robert Walpole provided money for the improvement of Aldridge's Lodge. Sixty years later the frontage was apparently remodelled by Soane, no doubt on the basis of his work on Pembroke Lodge and the Richmond Gate.

The building first appears as 'Thatched House Lodge' in a map of 1771, probably on account of the thatched summer house in the garden, which Walpole had constructed in 1727 to entertain fellow hunters, including the king, at the end of the chase. In the 1780s the interior of the Thatched House (composed of two octagonal rooms) was decorated, probably by the Venetian Antonio Zucchi (1726-95), husband of Angelica Kauffmann. Zucchi was Robert Adam's chief decorative painter. The paintings were removed for safekeeping in the 1960s. You may obtain a restricted view of the Thatched House by walking around the north side of the Lodge grounds.

Walk northwards, back towards Pembroke Lodge. Turn off to the right, down the carriageway to White Ash Lodge (1.5km).

White Ash Lodge was probably built at about the same time as Bog Lodge, in the 1730s or 1740s to accommodate the deputy keeper. It retains its charm, though the adjacent stable is in an advanced state of neglect. It will be recalled that James Sawyer had moved to Bog Lodge on his accession as head keeper in 1795. When he died in 1825 John Lucas, who had been too young to assume headship in 1795, was now invited to take up the post denied him then. Lucas apparently declined in favour of Sawyer's own son since he would have been obliged to move to Bog Lodge. He could not bear the thought of turning James Sawyer's widow and family out of the home they had enjoyed for 30 years. Apparently the two families lived intimately, frequently dining together. Both families were employed in the park for well over a century.

Return to Pembroke Lodge car park (1km).

Three other eighteenth century buildings, Ladderstile Cottage, Ham Gate Lodge and Bishop's Lodge are mentioned in Walk No. 6.

6 The Eighteenth Century Right of Access and Perimeter Walk

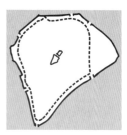

(14km/3 hours)

This walk tells the story of how the fight for public access was won and gives a brief outline of points of interest around the perimeter, including the origins of each gate.

In order to give a chronological account of the struggle for public access, this walk starts at Cambrian Gate. (However you may start from any gate you choose if you simply wish to walk the park perimeter, reading the relevant notes for each gate.) Turn left and make your way along the park wall for 400m to the stream that flows under the park wall.

Our right to walk in Richmond Park is in good measure thanks to a local man in the middle of the eighteenth century. Charles I had built a two-metre high wall to enclose the park but allowed complete freedom both to the public to cross the new park from one village or town to another and for the poor to gather firewood (presumably on the old medieval limitation of what could be gathered 'by hook or by crook'.) These liberalities were, no doubt, to avoid offending local people who had traditionally used the common pasture and woodland.

Six gates were put in the 1637 wall of enclosure, where the present Richmond, East Sheen, Roehampton, Robin Hood, Ladderstile and Ham Gates are located. Almost exactly a century

Keys and admission tickets to Richmond Park.

later access became progressively restricted and then virtually impossible in the 1750s. The present wall was probably built largely in the late eighteenth century, though it has been patched and repaired in many places since then.

The park had been enclosed to provide hunting for the king and his cronies. It was, perhaps, inevitable that local people with free access came to watch the royals at play, hunting stags and shooting wild turkey (with which the park was so liberally supplied, see Walk No. 5). In 1673 park gates had already been locked to prevent unauthorized farm livestock from grazing in the park. Ladderstiles were installed to allow people continued free access. By the mid-1730s so many people came to spectate that they were considered 'not only troublesome but very dangerous'. In 1735 George II's consort, Queen Caroline, authorised the issue of a notice to the effect that admittance in future would be allowed only to those with a 'hunting ticket' obtainable from the ranger. It was the carriage and mounted spectators who were the main problem, and many of

Beating the bounds of Richmond Parish, May 1751.

these had acquired their own keys to the gates. The locks were now changed, and some of the ladderstiles removed. In 1742 Walpole built lodges at the gates to admit 'all respectable persons' during daylight, but the restrictions were already creating considerable resentment in the locality.

In April 1751 Princess Amelia, George II's youngest daughter succeeded Lord Walpole as Ranger. Amelia was unusual, described by a contemporary as 'a masculine woman, fond of being in the stables, and an inveterate snufftaker'. In spite or because of these qualities she was her father's favourite daughter, but to the people surrounding the park she was a minx, for she resolved to make it wholly private.

Barely six weeks after her appointment, a Richmond Parish party, led by the vicar, made its annual Ascension Day ritual of beating the bounds of the parish, which included a slice of the park (see Nicholas Lane's map, page 10). When the party members had beaten the bounds as far as the park wall, precisely where the stream exits, they found to their dismay that not only was the bridle gate on the parish boundary locked as was normal (note the patched door-shaped section of wall just on the left of the stream probably where the bridle gate once was), but that the usual ladderstile was missing. Furthermore their progress was being observed by three men sitting on the wall. Whether the vicar, churchwarden and others actually broke part of the wall or climbed over a delapidated section, as a contemporary illustration suggests, they successfully entered the park, still closely observed by the same trio, now on horseback. Having beaten the bounds within the park, the party left by Richmond Gate, barely 50 metres from the point at which the parish boundary crosses the park wall on Star and Garter Hill.

It seems to have been the pretext Princess Amelia sought. For she now closed the park to all foot, horse and carriage traffic, only allowing her personal guests entry. Horace Walpole at Strawberry Hill watched with interest, particularly since his brother had preceded her as Park Ranger and his father had regularly hunted there:

> 'She preserved no measures of popularity....Petitions were presented to her, but she would not receive them; they were printed in the public newspapers but had as little effect.'

If there was any comfort at all for the local citizenry, it must have been that the nobility, too, was given short shrift, as Walpole wryly observed:

> 'Lord Brooke, who has taken the late Duchess of Rutland's [house] at Petersham, asked for a key. The answer was (mind it, for it was tolerably mortifying for an Earl) "that the Princess had already refused one to my Lord Chancellor."'

Every effort was made to shame the Princess into moderating her position. It was the mainly carriage-using gentry that brought the first court action against her, or rather against one of her gate keepers at Croydon Assizes in 1754, but they lost their case.

Proceed along the park wall towards East Sheen Gate, pausing at Bog Gate.

Bog Gate (or Queen's Gate): In 1736 the owners of Sheen Common issued a licence permitting Queen Caroline, George II's wife, to make a road to the 'new gate in the wall of the park' which had just been pierced for her. She used it as her private entrance for her journeys between Richmond Lodge (a royal residence in the Old Deer Park) and the White Lodge in the park. It became known as Bog Gate on account of a marshy area south east of the gate eventually drained in 1855. The Inns of Court Rifle Volunteers were permitted to use the gate in 1870 on their way to drill on the ground between the gate and Holly (Bog) Lodge. Militia membership was popular among young men at this time. Public access was granted 24 hours a day in 1894, and the present 'cradle' gate installed, probably the first for the park. At the end of the nineteenth century the metal-fenced enclosure on the west side of Bog Gate was used as the Richmond Rifle Club's range.

Proceed past Teck Plantation.

Kitchen Garden Gate, hidden behind Teck Plantation, is located at the western end of the Ranger's Garden. It is probably a nineteenth century gate and has never been used by the public. Teck Plantation commemorates the residence of the Duke and Duchess of Teck at the White Lodge. Their daughter became George V's consort, Queen Mary.

Proceed to East Sheen Gate.

Note on the left, set into the fencing of the present gate lodge, one of the old 'shelter boxes'. These were used by the 'Park Keeping Force', precursors of the Royal Parks Constabulary particularly in inclement weather. Another such lodge may be found towards the northern end of Pembroke Lodge Grounds, equipped with a fireplace and bookshelves. Nice to know they produced vulnerable as well as super humans in the age of empire. A police force was first established after a guest of the Russells walking through the park was relieved of her watch and jewellery at pistol point in 1854. Shelter boxes also existed by the barrow ((3) on Walk No. 1) above Ham Gate, and on the southern side of Spanker's Hill.

EAST SHEEN GATE: For anyone who values free use of the park this gate must be visited. For it was here in 1755 that John Lewis, a Richmond brewer, asserted the pedestrian right of entry after Princess Amelia had denied it. A contemporary friend and admirer of John Lewis, Gilbert Wakefield, recalled what happened:

'Lewis takes a friend with him to the spot, waits for the opportunity of a carriage passing through, and when the gatekeeper was shutting the gate, interposed and offered to go in. "Where is your ticket?" "What occasion for a ticket – anybody may pass through here?" "No, not without a ticket." "Yes, they may." "No, not without a ticket." "Yes, they may, and I will." "You shan't." "I will." The woman pushed; Lewis suffered the door to be shut upon him...'

Armed with the evidence of an eyewitness, John Lewis took his case against the gate keeper, Martha Gray, to the Kingston Assize. It took three years to get his case heard, but after a day's trial on 3 April 1758, the verdict went against the unfortunate Martha Gray. Wakefield continued:

'After the decree in his favour, Lewis was asked, whether he would have a step ladder to go over the wall, or a door? He hesitated for some minutes; but reflecting that strangers might not be aware of the privilege of admission through a door, which could not stand open on account of the deer; considering also that in process of time a bolt might be put on this door, and then a lock, and so his efforts be gradually frustrated; sensible too

that a step ladder, at the first inspection, would signify its use to
every beholder, he preferred that mode of introduction.'
On 12 May 1758 ladder-stiles were fixed to East Sheen and Ham
Gates, and on 16th May were thrown open, when 'a vast concourse
of people from all the neighbouring villages climbed over the
ladder stiles into the park.'

It was not quite the end of the story. John Lewis had to return to
court, for Princess Amelia tried to thwart its will by designing
ladders with the rungs spaced so far apart that the very young and
the old could not get up them. She was tersely instructed by the
court to provide ladders that were easy to climb.

Such was John Lewis' celebrity that his portrait was painted by
Thomas Stewart, a pupil of Sir Joshua Reynolds. (Reynolds,
incidentally, lived at Wick House on Richmond Hill's Terrace.) The
painting now hangs in Richmond Reference Library, and an
engraving made with the following incription by Gilbert's brother,
Thomas Wakefield the vicar
of St Mary Magdalene, the
parish church of Richmond:

> 'Be it remembered That by
> the steady Perseverance
> of John Lewis, Brewer, at
> Richmond Surry, the
> Right of a Free Passage
> through Richmond Park
> was recovered after being
> upwards of twenty Years
> withheld from the People.'

Carriage owners were now
emboldened to bring their
own case in 1760 for use of
the carriage and bridleways,

John Lewis by Thomas Stewart

but they were again unsuccessful. By now, however, Princess Amelia's local standing could hardly have been worse and she resigned the Rangership the following year. On assuming the office of Ranger himself in 1792, George III relaxed the prohibition on carriages. The present double gates date from 1926.

Proceed to Roehampton Gate.

Patches and irregularities in the wall 200m from East Sheen Gate mark the remains of Sheen Cottage (see Walk No. 9).

Note also approaching Roehampton Gate major surface drainage ditches running to the park wall. The original ditches were probably part of George III's endeavours at the end of the eighteenth century.

ROEHAMPTON GATE: One of the six original gates. For part of the nineteenth century and probably previously, the park authorities had to pay a quit rent of one buck a year for the right of way, as the gate opened upon private property. The present wrought iron carriage gates date from 1899.

Follow the path beside Beverley Brook to Robin Hood Gate, since the land north of Beverley Brook, including Chohole Gate is inaccessible except to golfers.

Beverley Brook rises at Worcester Park and enters the Thames at Barn Elms Park, Putney. Sadly, in dry weather about 90 per cent of the flow is provided by effluent from Worcester Park Sewage Treatment Works but this, too, is traditional, for in the seventeenth century it was known as 'the common sewer'. It still manages to sustain a few sticklebacks, enough to entice one or two kingfishers.

[CHOHOLE GATE: Lies in the extreme south east corner of the park. It is first mentioned in 1680 when a warrant was issued 'to cause the grass now growing in the paddock near Chohole Gate to be cut and sold, same being coarse and not fit food for the deer.' The gate probably takes its name from the charcoal which may once have been burnt near here and removed through it. It served the farm which stood within the park on the site of the present Kingsfarm Plantation.]

ROBIN HOOD GATE: One of the six original gates. It was probably first called Wimbledon Gate, but by the mid-eighteenth century was already known as Robin Hood Gate on account of the proximity of the Robin Hood Inn. It was widened in 1907.

At the foot of Broomfield Hill note the patch of gorse protected by a railing, practically all that is left of the extensive gorse cover when the park was enclosed. There are two other patches of gorse (i) between Conduit Wood and Holly (Bog) Lodge, and (ii) another fenced patch on the south side of Spankers Hill. Even a century ago there were large tracts of gorse in the enclosed preserves in the park, but once these were thrown open the gorse bushes were progressively eliminated, since the deer are partial to its young and tender shoots.

At the top of Broomfield Hill, towards Ladderstile Gate, a section of wall was removed in the nineteenth century and replaced by a ha-ha, to afford a parkland vista following the construction of the Italianate Kingston Hill Place in 1828. On the north east side of the ha-ha are traces of a bridle gate that existed in the mid-eighteenth century and seems to have been bricked up sometime in the nineteenth century. Lily Langtry lived here, but one must doubt that her friendship with Edward, Prince of Wales, which flourished

in the 1880s involved the White Lodge, since the Tecks were in
residence there from 1869-1899.

LADDERSTILE GATE: one of the six original gates, it was known as
Coombe Gate and provided access for the parishioners of Coombe
(now commemorated in the name 'Coombe Road' running from
Kingston to Raynes Park). During the first court action of 1754 the
gate figured in the evidence. There had been both a gate and a step
ladder. The gate had been locked in the early years of the century
and actually bricked up in about 1735. Among the evidence
produced in 1754 was the remarkable fact that

> 'Mr Hervey, late of Comb Park, was deprived of his key [to
> Ladderstile Gate] and in revenge planted French wheat in the
> adjacent lands, by which he enticed over the Pheasants, and
> killed ten brace in a day.'

The step ladder was reinstated after John Lewis' test case in 1758
and remained until about 1884, long after the other stepladders
around the park had disappeared (except at Ham), hence it became
popularly known as Ladderstile Gate about 1850. The present gate
dates from 1901.

Ladderstile Gate had one moment of notoriety. At 3am on
17 April 1874 a desperate encounter took place between a local
burglar, George Offord, and Police Constable Kerrison. Offord
discharged a revolver at PC Kerrison before climbing up the
ladderstile. Kerrison bravely pursued him but was struck over the
head with the revolver butt. Despite serious head injuries Kerrison
hung onto Offord's leg until help came and Offord was
overpowered.

Ladderstile Cottage was built in the 1780s.

KINGSTON GATE: was not one of the original six park gates and
only seems to have come into existence in about 1750. In 1861

Queen Victoria opened a new pair of iron gates, opened to foot passengers all night from 1877. The existing gate dates from 1898.

HAM GATE: One of the original six gates. The gate lodge, the only surviving original, was built in 1742. A ladderstile survived until 1850 or so. The present gate was widened in 1921 and the present wrought iron gates substituted for the previous wooden ones. Note the chinoiserie lantern lights over the gate installed in 1825, still lit by gas.

Follow the Sudbrook (just beyond Ham Gate Pond).

Note the ancient pollarded willows on its banks.

Skirt the edge of Sudbrook Park.

Most of Sudbrook Park had been acquired piecemeal by John, 2nd Duke of Argyll, but the lease of about 30 acres of the park was granted by George I in 1726. This made possible the construction by James Gibbs of the fine mansion across the old park boundary, visible across the present golf course, in 1728. Hence no wall exists along this stretch of the park perimeter. Gibbs, incidentally, is best known for St Martin-in-the-Fields and St Mary-le-Strand in London, Oxford's Radcliffe Camera and the Fellows Building, King's College, Cambridge. Argyll's estate now extended up to Pembroke Lodge on the escarpment and abutted Petersham Park to the north. A few bricks and stones are all that remain of a small reservoir half way up the hill, which used to supply Sudbrook Park with water. Part of the Sudbrook estate subsequently reverted to the Crown and was reintegrated into the park. The golf club was established in 1891.

PETERSHAM GATE: A large ornamental gate served Petersham Lodge from 1686. After Petersham Park was reintegrated into the Richmond Park in 1833, a pedestrian gate replaced it, which served the Russell School (see Walk No. 9). The carriage gate a few metres up the hill was probably the tradesmen's access to the school, or was once access to the stables of Petersham Lodge.

Petersham Hill: Half way up, there is a permanently locked foot gate. There is also a stretch of wall where the brickwork was replaced by railings in 1843, nine years after the reincorporation of Petersham Park, to provide a vista onto Petersham Common from the terrace walk above.

RICHMOND GATE: is one of the original six gates and seems always to have borne the heaviest traffic. The present gate and lodge bearing the cyphers GR (George III) and CR (his consort Queen Charlotte) was erected in 1798, almost certainly to a design by Sir John Soane (original drawings in the Soane Museum, Lincoln's Inn Fields). The gates were widened in 1896. According to a guide book dated 1824:

> 'Large iron gates open to receive carriages into its domains. Upon ringing a bell and producing an order from the deputy ranger, Lord Sidmouth, the keeper at the lodge, remarkable for his civility, appears for your admission.'

Princess Amelia would have been mortified.

Beside Richmond Gate stands Ancaster House, now the residence of the Commandant of the Star and Garter Home. It was built in 1772 by the Duke of Ancaster. It was then acquired by a baronet, Sir Lionel Darell. Darell found the park wall oppressively close to his house and wanted a larger garden. How he succeeded illustrates perfectly that it is *who* you know not what you know that counts. At first he went through all the correct channels, applying to the Lords of the Treasury and the Commissioners of Crown Lands, to no avail since both offices found one reason after another to demur and delay. Ever had that feeling? Always go to the top. When George III was riding past one day and bade him good day, Darell seized his chance. 'How much do you want?' asked the king. When Darell showed him his modest intentions, the king expostulated, 'Are you sure that will be enough? Don't stint yourself.' Fortunately for us Darell did not have the presence of mind to request another 50 acres. George dismounted and marked out a line himself with a stick, saying 'There you are, that is your ground, it is mine no longer.' Hence Darell removed the wall, and railings mark his slightly enlarged garden.

BISHOP'S (Chisholm Road) GATE: previously consisting of two large wooden gates, the Cattle Gate, as it used to be known, was for livestock allowed to pasture in the park in the nineteenth century. It was not opened to the public until 1896, as a result of a petition from those living in Chisholm Road and nearby. Bishop's Gate is one of the only places where one may still see the 16.5 ft freebord of Crown property that runs (invisibly) around most of the park. It is the dog-leg through to Chisholm Road.

Bishop's Lodge, built into the wall at Bishop's Gate towards the end of the eighteenth century, was probably named after two assistant keepers, William Bishop and his son Charles, employed between 1790-1830, approximately.

CAMBRIAN ROAD GATE: This gate was constructed for the convenience of the South Africa Military Hospital (Walk No. 9) during the First World War. When the latter was demolished in 1925, the entrance was made permanent and public as a cradle gate.

The park in the nineteenth century

In spite of winning the battle for public access in 1758, pedestrians were still expected to keep to the footpaths, and carriages were required to obtain admission cards until the 1850s. The map on page 80, produced in 1876, indicates that even after visitors were encouraged to enjoy the park, substantial portions of the park were still designated as Preserves, or for special use.

Yet Richmond Park did begin to change, ceasing to be a hunting park and becoming more of a pleasurable place to promenade. This was thanks largely to two men, Lord Sidmouth and Edward Jesse. As mentioned in the preceding walk, in 1813 George III (the first monarch to hold the Rangership personally) made Sidmouth his Deputy Ranger, effectively his park manager. Sidmouth, already at the White Lodge, dined Walter Scott, Pitt the Younger, Richard Sheridan who lived at Downe House on the Terrace, and most notably in 1804 Lord Nelson who apparently dipped his finger in his wine glass to trace out his battle plan for destroying the French fleet on the dining table at White Lodge, a manoeuvre duly executed the following year at Trafalgar.

Sidmouth conceived a passion for trees, and initiated a programme of tree planting that continued throughout the century long after his death in 1844. How far the park had become depleted of trees is difficult to say, and it may be that all Sidmouth and his successors did was to ensure the park remained amply stocked. But from Sidmouth onwards, tree planting became a central consideration in administration of the park, with major plantings in the 1820 and 1830s, and again in the 1870s and 1880s. Most of the plantations were fenced in to protect them from the deer and the fences only removed after Edward VII's decision in 1906 to make all parts of the park accessible to the public.

Sidmouth himself had two priorities, to create a number of closely planted woods in the body of the park, and also to conceal much of the park perimeter behind trees. Perhaps he anticipated the urbanisation that took place around the perimeter from about 1850 onwards.

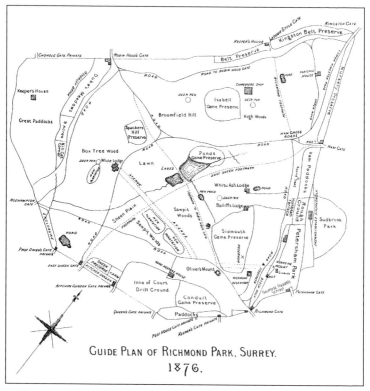

Richmond Park in 1876

7 *The Nineteenth Century Short Walk*

(6km/1.5 hour)

If you wish to walk further, Walk No 8 provides a longer version.

Start at the Pen Ponds Car Park.

Sidmouth started in 1819 by planting a section of trees on Spankers Hill on the east side of the car park, enlarged in 1824 and again in 1877.

Between the car park and the Upper Pen Pond lies Lawn Plantation, one of the last 19th century plantations (1883), and a good example of some of the smaller tree clusters subsequently planted. ('Lawn' or 'laund', incidentally, is old English for a stretch of untilled ground or a woodland clearing.)

Proceed westwards along the road towards Ham Cross.

On your right the south west end of the Pen Pond, Pond Plantation, was planted in 1865. It remains fenced as a water fowl preserve. On your right, Isabella Plantation, planted from 1831, is also still fenced, to protect its woodland garden from the deer (see Walk No. 11).

After almost 1 km turn right at the cross paths at the end of Pen Pond Plantation, crossing Pond Slade.

Besides Lord Sidmouth, the other nineteenth century figure of note was the naturalist Edward Jesse, Surveyor of HM Parks and Palaces, who recorded his observations of Richmond Park in his *Gleanings of Natural History* (London, 1834-35). Jesse's two major contributions concerned the quality of the land and the size of the park. Jesse was anxious to increase venison production, and in a survey in 1831 he recommended yet another major effort be made to drain the boggy areas of the park in order to provide better grazing. There had been numerous attempts in the past to drain boggy areas, notably the works carried out by Edward Manning at the time of the enclosure, and by George III at the end of the eighteenth century. Jesse's recommendation was not immediately implemented, no doubt because previous efforts had been so unsuccessful. Two areas in particular acutely needed draining. Pond Slade, which you are now crossing, and the area north and north east of Holly (Bog) Lodge.

Jesse's recommendation was revived in the 1850s because of the spreading fame of a new drainage expert, Josiah Parkes (1793-1871). Traditionally land drains were relatively shallow, in the belief that achieving good run-off would ensure that the land would not become waterlogged. Parkes, however, had noticed that his experimental deep drains began to run after wet weather not from the water above but from the water rising from subterranean accumulation below, and that by draining the stagnant moisture from 4 foot below the surface, the soil was rendered more friable and porous. In 1856 he was commissioned to design and implement a system of drains for about two thirds of the park – a job completed in 1861, together with the construction of 9 new ponds (listed on p.131) as watering for the deer. Parkes' work was largely successful. The land became better drained, leading to improved grazing for the deer herds. However, his drains silted up in due course. Ensuring satisfactory land drains remains a perennial task.

Take the path forking left after 200m and make for White Ash Lodge, go round the back of it and follow its drive out to the main carriageway. Cross it and 75m on opposite side turn right

into the Hornbeam Walk (glance to your left to enjoy the vista of the Walk).

The Hornbeam Walk was probably planted in the 1840s, a deliberate move in the conversion of the park from a place of desperate chases into one for pleasant promenades. Note Oak Lodge on your right (half hidden in the southern corner of Sidmouth Plantation) built in the early 1850s to accommodate the park bailiff, responsible for general maintenance of the park.

At the end of the Hornbeam Walk (200m) enter Pembroke Lodge grounds through the wicket gate, walk round to the terrace overlooking the Thames Valley.

This is a suitable moment for a small historical diversion. It will be recalled from Walk No.5 that Lord John Russell (1792-1878) moved into Pembroke Lodge in 1847. Russell had made his name championing the passage of the Reform Bill of 1832. He came from an aristocratic family (the dukes of Bedford) noted for its public spirit. His own liberal inclinations were probably also due to a private education rather than attendance at a public school and, eschewing Oxbridge, his attendance at Edinburgh university where he imbibed the philosophy of the Scottish Enlightenment. He championed the cause of religious freedom for English Dissenters and Irish Catholics, but as prime minister his attempts to end civil disabilities for Jews, extend the franchise to urban workers and guarantee security of tenure to Irish farmers were frustrated by party disunity. Thwarted in public life, he retreated to Pembroke Lodge where he wrote copiously – poetry, biography and history – till his death.

Pembroke Lodge was also the childhood home of his grandson, Bertrand Russell. He arrived at the age of four, and the opening sentence of his autobiography reads 'My first vivid recollection is my arrival at Pembroke Lodge in February 1876.' Both parents died before he was four. Contrary to his parents' wish for him to be brought up by atheistic friends, he became the ward of his grandmother, Lady Russell, a woman of strict personal conscience and Puritan views, and so grew up at Pembroke Lodge, where

'Throughout the greater part of my childhood, the most important hours of my day were those that I spent in the garden.....I knew each corner of the garden, and looked year by year for the white primroses in one place, the redstart's nest in another, the blossom of the acacia emerging from a tangle of ivy. I knew where the earliest bluebells were to be found, and which of the oaks came into leaf soonest....'

One of his great childhood friends was Annabel Grant Duff, who lived at York House, Twickenham. In a memoir of her early life, she wrote:

'My only boy friend was Bertrand Russell..... Bertie and I were great allies and I had a secret admiration for his beautiful and gifted elder brother Frank. Frank, I am sorry to say, sympathized with my brother's point of view about little girls and used to tie me up to trees by my hair. But Bertie, a solemn little boy in a blue velvet suit with an equally solemn governess, was always kind, and I greatly enjoyed going to tea at Pembroke Lodge. But even as a child I realized what an unsuitable place it was for children to be brought up in. Lady Russell always spoke in hushed tones and Lady Agatha always wore a white shawl and looked down-trodden.... They all drifted in and out of the rooms like ghosts and no one ever seemed to be hungry. It was a curious bringing up for two young and extraordinarily gifted boys.'

Educated privately, Russell became intensely interested, in his own words, in 'how much we can be said to know and with what degree of certainty or doubtfulness.' The rest, as they say, is history, as he became internationally celebrated as philosopher, pacifist and campaigner against nuclear weaponry. In the prologue to his autobiography, he wrote:

> 'Three passions, simple but overwhelmingly strong, have governed my life: the longing for love, the search for knowledge, and unbearable pity for the suffering of mankind.'

Nice to think – in spite of Annabel Grant Duff's assessment – of Pembroke Lodge as the cradle for such greatness.

And now back to earth.

Descend from the terrace and turn right out of the gate at the bottom of the garden. You are now walking along the old perimeter of Petersham Park.

It will be recalled from Walk No. 4 that Charles II had granted the Petersham section of the park along with the Keepership to the Countess of Dysart (hence the eponymous Petersham pub); that in 1683 the Earl of Rochester had been granted a personal lease over a 50 acre plot, and that his magnificent mansion, 'New Park', had been destroyed by fire in 1721; that eleven years later Lord Burlington had designed a new lodge for Lord Harrington.

By the end of the eighteenth century the property, now about 100 acres in size, was in the hands of Lord Huntingtower (another Dysart). This large estate stretched all the way from the park wall at the bottom of the hill up to Pembroke Lodge and the fence running along the escarpment to Richmond Gate.

Jesse had had his eye on Petersham Park and when Lord Huntingtower died in 1833 he pursuaded his principals to buy Petersham Park for £14,500 and reintegrate it into Richmond Park. Petersham Lodge, already virtually derelict, was demolished in 1835. Trees of the parkland (or their descendants) still festoon the hillside, including old Lebanon cedars, then probably only seedlings. For the Russell school, which stood beside Petersham Gate, see Walk No 9.

Proceed along the western (just under the escarpment) edge of Pembroke Lodge Grounds for about 600m, pass on your right a nineteenth century brick domed artesian well-house, and after another 200m turn right at the cross path up a very steep slippery slope (there were steps here only 20 years ago) through rhododendrons, with a metal fence on your right, back on to the escarpment.

At the top you will cross Jesse's 'New Terrace' or Beech Walk. This is less successful than the Hornbeam Walk, but was intended to provide a pleasant walk (where none had previously existed) from Richmond Gate to Pembroke Lodge with splendid views across the recently re-integrated Petersham parkland. Jesse had many of the trees cleared from Petersham Park and from the old boundary fence in order to provide a view of the river from the Beech Walk. It was also at about this time that railings replaced the wall on Star and Garter Hill in order to give a view across Petersham Meadow. These views have now been lost due to foliage growth. Furthermore, while some beeches have been replanted the walk now lacks the coherence one suspects was originally intended.

Strike off half right in the direction of Sidmouth wood, and as you approach it, note a raised area with manhole covers.

This is a covered reservoir, one of two built in 1875-76, with Queen Victoria's consent, to supply Richmond with pumped Thames water. In 1860 Richmond had agreed to the supply of water by Southwark and Vauxhall Water Company, in spite of its relatively high prices. In 1873 S&V doubled its prices for water that proved to be badly polluted, and it was decided to replace its expensive services with locally supplied water. With this in mind two reservoirs were constructed (the other is in Sidmouth Wood, just behind the section of feather-edged fencing opposite Pembroke

Lodge car park). S&V refused to allow its own mains network to be used. Before the reservoirs were finished or houses re-connected, S&V cut off its supply in January 1877. For a month water was brought into Richmond mainly by water bowser, a major source of water being Leg of Mutton Pond (still then known as the Pen Pond, between Sidmouth Wood and the Pen Ponds), which produced purer water, so it was claimed, than S&V.

Follow the edge of Sidmouth Wood southwards 200m to the wicket gate leading into the Driftway.

Sidmouth's memorial, of course, is the wood named after him. The north-western tip was planted in 1823, and the rest in 1830. The vista through the avenue of trees from King Henry VIII's mound was preserved as a cutting through the plantation (to be admired on Walk No. 1). During the third quarter of the nineteenth century the wood was used as a pheasant cover. The Driftway itself was only opened to the public in 1906.

On emerging from the Driftway veer around the northern tip of Queen Elizabeth's Plantation, past the Leg of Mutton Pond, (admiring but preferably not testing its potable quality) back to the Pen Pond car park.

8 *The Nineteenth Century Long Walk*

(9km/2.5 hours)

This is an extended version of Walk No. 7.

Start at Sheen Wood car park (East Sheen Gate).

Sheen Wood, along with Spanker's Hill the first of Lord Sidmouth's plantations, was the beginning of his plan to obscure much of the park wall. In 1825 he planted trees from Sheen Cottage, 200m east of East Sheen Gate (see Walk No. 9), to Roehampton Gate, and the following year trees along the wall from Kingston Vale over the hill to Kingston Gate. At the same time he planted more trees along Ham Bottom from Kingston Gate to Ham Gate.

Walk towards Roehampton Gate following the plantation, but turn southwards when you reach Beverley Brook and make for the woods behind (east of) The White Lodge.

White Lodge Wood is representative of the 1870s programme intended to thicken up thinly wooded areas. This area was originally planted when cultivation was abandoned, probably in the fourteenth century. The wooden deer pen on the north east slopes of White Lodge wood is the only one surviving from the nineteenth century. There was originally a smaller pen inside that could only be entered by fawns/calves. This was to ensure they obtained sufficient supplementary food.

Continue walking due south through Treebox Wood (1877) and around the east and southern side of Spankers Hill Wood.

Spankers Hill Wood was planted between 1819-24, around Hartleton (The Old) Lodge which was still standing.

Pass the Pen Ponds car park on your right and follow Walk No 7, until you have walked through the Sidmouth Wood Driftway and emerged on the south east side. Now turn left (but not hard left) and walk 500m across the hillside, crossing the major path running down to the Pen Ponds, until you reach the Queen's Ride.

At the west end of the Queen's Ride, close to the tenth tree on its northern side, there is a Mortlake Parish boundary stone dated 1857. It is difficult to spot.

Walk down the Queen's Ride, skirt around Saw Pit Plantation, and turn northwards, back to Sheen Cross, and thence back to Sheen Wood car park.

The Twentieth Century

It may seem surprising in an age of self-conscious conservation that the park has undergone greater changes during the present century than in any preceding one. This is primarily the result of two world wars, but also from the conscious decision by Edward VII to develop the park as a public amenity. He ordered the opening of virtually all the previously fenced woods, the only substantial exceptions being Sidmouth Wood (but public access to the Driftway was established), Pond Plantation (as a bird sanctuary) and Teck Plantation near East Sheen Gate, and private gates were made public for the benefit of the greatly increased local population. It was the act of an increasingly 'middle class' monarchy for the new, demanding, and predominantly middle class suburbs. From 1915 level areas of the park were marked out for football and cricket pitches, presumably for the troops as well as local clubs. No less than 40 such pitches existed by 1939. In 1923 the golf course was opened by the Prince of Wales for those – in fact 'local artisans' – who could not afford membership of a private club, another example of the new 'popular' monarchy.

The effects of world war were threefold: military camps and hospitals were constructed in the park; over a quarter of the park was either put under cultivation (mainly around East Sheen Gate) or used as grazing; and certain buildings were destroyed by enemy action. F. D. Ommaney, who spent his youth in Sheen Cottage (see below) recalled of the First War:

'Every holiday, when I returned home, the ugly evidences of war spread farther and wider over the green spaces around the house in the park. For several centuries it had looked out upon scenes of immemorial peace. Now, from the warlike clamour that increased around it, it seemed to shrink back among the trees. Rows of huts sprang up and the inevitable cookhouses and latrines accompanied them. Guns pushed up their snouts among the trees. Army lorries, disregarding the sacred rules enforced upon us for years by stately old gentlemen in top hats with gold braid around them [the park police], careered across the green levels and scarred them with their wheels. In the plantations they stood in rows like prehistoric monsters asleep. Captive balloons hung above, obese shapes in our familiar sky. Columns of soldiers marched and drilled, attracting from the purlieus down the hill troops of raffish vivandières, who wandered about in groups and made sly giggling invitations. The sound of rifle fire and bursting grenades echoed among the copses.'

During the Second World War the Pen Ponds themselves were drained to disguise so prominent a landmark.

The remarkable fact is that at the end of the century, apart from the loss of pre-war buildings, it is only an informed eye that will

The London Scottish marching into camp, 1915

detect where these activities were. Most traces have been carefully erased. The real transformation of the park from the arcadian retreat it once was results from the relentless traffic crossing it during the daylight hours and the noise of aircraft approaching or leaving Heathrow Airport. Both seriously diminish the quality of Richmond Park.

Richmond Park was also the scene of wartime innovation. In November 1917 trials were carried out on H. G. Wells' 'aerial ropeway'. Far from being a batty brainstorm, Wells had evolved this way of moving rations, ammunition, equipment and wounded men, following the death of hundreds of men carrying rations and ammunition up to the front line in the Third Battle of Ypres. Some had died under enemy fire, others had slipped off the duckboards and drowned in flooded shell craters. Wells' ropeway was designed to be erected after dark for night use. It was hung on 10' poles and could convey 10 tons per hour for a distance of half a mile. But the generals turned it down. Wells commented, 'the tin hats did not like it', bitterly deriding them as 'fine, handsome, well-groomed, neighing gentlemen' with 'clear definite ideas of what war was.'

In the Second World War, the park was used for special forces. GHQ (Phantom) Liaison Regt trained here, the actor David Niven among them. The regiment suffered 50 per cent casualties, for they were used as scouts to locate the enemy. During the retreat to Dunkirk it is said they spent more time trying to find the French than the enemy. Some personnel were used as 'listeners' either forward of the front line or parachuted behind enemy lines to eavesdrop on German wireless transmissions.

9 *The Twentieth Century Walk*

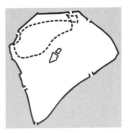

(6.5km/1.5 hours or
11km/2.5 hours)

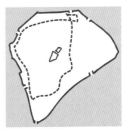

Start at Sheen Wood car park (East Sheen Gate). Turn east (left) and walk 150m along the wall.

Traces of Sheen Cottage are discernible on the park wall, which has been extensively patched. It was originally built against the park wall probably in the 1720s by Sir Robert Walpole for his huntsman and deerhounds, and was marked on eighteenth century maps simply as 'Dog Kennel'. With the end of

Sheen Cottage

deerhunting in the middle of the century the house was occupied by one of the park under-keepers. But in about 1787 a William Adam obtained permission to occupy part of the house, and then paid the under-keeper compensation to vacate the whole property. Adam, who became High Commissioner for Scotland during George IV's reign, his son, who became Accountant General of the Court of Chancery, and then his two grandsons all occupied the house until 1852. The house was enlarged along the wall. It had one garden inside the park and another outside it. It is from Adam that the nearby pond derives its name.

Sir Richard Owen, eminent anatomist, palaeontologist and first Director of the Natural History Museum, was the next occupant of Sheen Cottage, until his death in 1892. In the words of his great grandson, F. D. Ommaney:

'He expounded the manners and habits of beasts.....his wife...recorded.... how he brought back the remains of a hippopotamus from the Zoo to dissect at home, filling the house with too-African odours. A faint note of protest was perceptible in the patient diary......

'The old man lived in this house until he died at a great age – over ninety. He..... was a dominating and masterful spirit with great personal charm, which he could turn on and off like a tap, and a biting sarcastic humour which he apparently reserved for his large family circle.'

Threatened in his position as Britain's pre-eminent biologist, Owen anonymously attacked his old friend Charles Darwin's *Origin of Species*, following its publication in 1859. Darwin responded:

'It is extremely malignant, clever, and I fear will be very damaging...It requires much study to appreciate all the bitter spite of many of the remarks against me....He misquotes some passages, altering words within inverted commas...'

You may still find traces of the old building and garden, the highlight of your researches being the site of the household's flush lavatory. It was destroyed, the cottage that is, by enemy action in 1944.

Pick up the riding track just south of Adams Pond and follow it westwards, past Holly (Bog) Lodge to Bishops Pond (2km).

Virtually the whole area between Conduit Wood and Bishop's Pond was the site of the South Africa Military Hospital, built during the First World War close to Cambrian Road, where the park wall was pierced to allow access (see Walk No. 6). The hospital extended over 12 acres, and was composed of rows of wooden huts on brick piers, designed 'after the manner of South African colonial timber-framed dwellings'. One may easily imagine

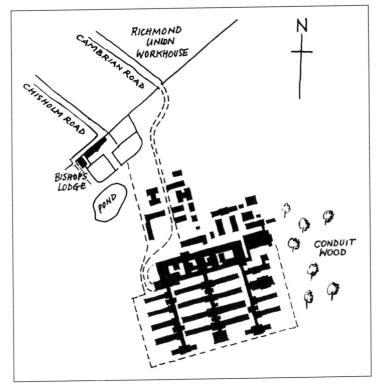

Layout of the hospital

Main entrance to the South African War Hospital

the horse-drawn ambulances making their laborious way up from Richmond Station with their pain-wracked loads.

The hospital facilities were said to be the most advanced of their kind in Britain, and included 'bath-beds' – the only ones of their kind in Britain – for those with bad shell wounds or advanced septicaemia. The patient would recline on a cradle suspended in flowing water at body temperature. This treatment, normally lasting 4-5 days, greatly eased the pain otherwise incurred by changing dressings, helped drain septic wounds and made sleep easier. However, the South African Forces section of Richmond Cemetery bears melancholy testimony to the large number of young men who failed to make it – a powerful reminder of the pity of war.

The hospital was assigned to the Ministry of Pensions at the end of the war and only demolished in 1925. During dry summer weather one can still see the outline of the earthworks connected with the hospital on the ground used as an informal football pitch.

The Russell School in the late nineteenth century

Walk to Richmond Gate, and follow the wall down to Petersham Gate (1km).

The Russell School stood beside the gate, at the very foot of the hill. It was established by Lady Russell of Pembroke Lodge (see Walk No. 7) in a room in Petersham in 1849 and two years later moved into the new building just inside Petersham Gate. The new schoolhouse contained three classrooms, for infants, middles and seniors which, as one ex-pupil recalled, '.....sloped steeply to the back, with steps which tripped the unwary.' In the summer most lessons took place under the fir trees, the park itself being 'our delight..... the most perfect of all playgrounds.' The schoolhouse was destroyed by enemy action in 1943. It was rebuilt on the Petersham Road. Nothing remains of the original school.

To return to East Sheen Gate: proceed through Petersham Park, climbing back on to the escarpment at the south end of Pembroke Lodge, skirting the south side of Sidmouth Wood, across the Queen's Ride, through Sawpit Plantation, and past Barn Wood Pond (3.5km);

OR

If you are feeling energetic, continue walking through Petersham Park and Ham Bottom, climbing the escarpment on the south side of Thatched House Lodge (2.5km). (This part may be done as a separate outing from Kingston or Ladderstile Gates, or Broomfield Hill Car park).

You are now on the edge of Kingston Gate Camp, an army hutted camp established in 1938 to house conscripts of the East Surrey Regiment. It was subsequently used as a military convalescent depot, then by the women's army unit, the Auxiliary Territorial Service (ATS) and after the war by its successor unit, the Women's Royal Army Corps (WRAC). It was used as an extremely cramped and spartan Olympic Village in 1948, and as a hostel for service families evacuated from the Suez Canal Zone in 1956. It was dismantled in 1965 and re-integrated into the park in the summer of 1966. There are plenty of people around who remember it. It was extensive, occupying an area on the northern side of the Kingston-Robin Hood Gate carriageway from Dark Hill/King's Clump, across to Thatched House Lodge, and up to Dann's Pond. One can still see earthworks including the covered remains of a tennis court just east of Thatched House Lodge. The only surviving surface evidence of the camp is a flight of eight concrete steps (if you can find them).

Follow the track past Dann's Pond, and around the south east side of Isabella Plantation (Walk No. 11) and go through the

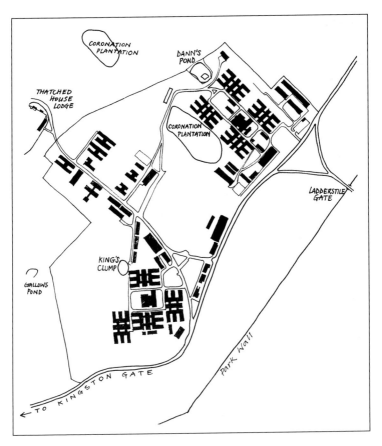

Kingston Gate Camp

cutting across Prince Charles Spinney.

The spinney was planted in 1951, three years after his birth.

Emerge from the spinney and bear left, pass Pen Ponds car park, and follow the carriageway back past the White Lodge and East Sheen Gate (or if you have made this a separate walk, return to your start point.)

Manorial and parish boundaries

INTRODUCTION

Visible traces of the old manorial and parish boundaries are meagre. A pattern of parishes, the ecclesiastical administration of England, was well established by 1000. Most parish boundaries, even in the remoter parts of England had been drawn by the end of the twelfth century. By the fifteenth century there were some 10,000 parishes in England and theoretically these became units of civil administration, rather than solely ecclesiastical units, in the sixteenth century.

Yet in practice the medieval manor remained a more important unit of administration until well into the seventeenth century. As noted in Walk No. 4, leases and holdings were still recorded in terms of manor boundaries, and these are what were marked on maps of the time.

However, the tradition of 'beating the parish bounds' every Ascension Day began to be established during the reign of Elizabeth I, from older ceremonies of Rogationtide. Although originally a religious ceremony, beating the bounds had two functions: to ensure that the boundaries of the parish had not been infringed and if so, to challenge that infringement (as is clear from the incident of 1751 described in Walk No. 6) and to instil in the minds of all villagers, particularly the young, the exact limits of the parish. The parson would lead his parishioners around the boundary in procession, stopping at certain oak trees to offer prayers for good crops (thus known as 'gospel oaks'). Some oaks were planted specifically as boundary marks, particularly where the boundary suddenly changed direction. Elsewhere stones were used. Both oaks and stones were used as boundary marks in

Richmond Park. Unfortunately, most of these boundaries have been amended at least once in the intervening period since the sixteenth century. However, although parishes gave way to boroughs as units of administration (Richmond in 1890, for example), Ordnance Survey maps published earlier this century still showed oak trees that marked parish boundaries some of which must still be standing but, having lost whatever defining marks they once had, are extraordinarily difficult to identify. One of the only surviving parish boundary stones (on the Mortlake-Petersham border) features in Walk No. 8, on p.89.

10 *Richmond Parish Boundary*

(2km/40 minutes)

This boundary is clearly marked – as 'Richmond Comon' – on Lane's map, and may easily be followed. You will be following a boundary that may date back to the twelfth century or even earlier, whenever the manorial demesne of Shene was actually established.

Enter the park at Richmond Gate.

The old boundary with Petersham enters the park just on the right, behind the public lavatories at the point where railings replace the full height park wall on Star and Garter Hill, and runs almost straight to the convex curve of the north-western edge of Sidmouth Wood.

Begin walking along the north side of the Richmond-Kingston carriageway.

Almost immediately there is large old oak (100 paces from the roundabout) probably a marker oak on the old parish boundary line.

Strike off slightly to the left of the carriageway and walk through the middle of Kidney Wood and make for the concave NW edge of Sidmouth wood.

The left hand wooden bench on the track skirting Sidmouth Wood is approximately where a large boundary oak stood 150 years ago, marking the apex of the wedge of Richmond parish common land falling within the park, and where the parishes of Petersham, Richmond and Mortlake met.

Turn east-north-east and start walking towards Conduit Wood following the lowest ground as it begins to become a gully, and then an open stream leading through the heart of Conduit Wood.

This is the line of the old parish boundary with Mortlake.

Follow the stream through the wood, out the far side and down to the park wall.

This stream was the parish border. On the edge of the boggy area 75m below Conduit Wood, one may find a half-buried stone outcrop which may be the remains of another pre-enclosure conduit house (see Walk No. 4 for the White Conduit, the brick structure in Conduit Wood).

The stream turns left for the last 200 metres or so before reaching the park wall. This can be seen quite distinctly on Lane's map and appears to mark one side of Humphry Bennet's holding. Note the willows on the right bank, which are planted in straight lines along what may have been drainage ditches. It is unclear how long they have been there, but they indicate a field boundary at least 150 years old.

Just on the left of the culvert where the stream leaves the park, the wall clearly once had a doorway, now patched. The assumption must be that this was a doorway once used to beat the bounds.

OTHER BOUNDARIES

Unfortunately other boundaries are much harder to follow:

1. MORTLAKE-PETERSHAM boundary ran from the north edge of Sidmouth Wood where there is a Mortlake boundary stone hidden in the rhododendrons just inside the metal fence, across to the west end of Sawpit Plantation. A boundary stone may be found, marked 'MP [Mortlake Parish] 1857', standing beside the tenth tree on the north side of the Queen's Ride. The boundary ran to another stone now buried in the bracken on the hill overlooking the Lower Pen Pond and then in a straight line down to the pond. At this point it became the boundary between Mortlake and Ham.

2. THE MORTLAKE-HAM boundary crossed the Lower Pen Pond, and curved over the saddle between Spanker's and White Lodge hills to skirt the northern edge of Treebox Wood. This last section is traceable.

If you wish to find it, leave your car at Robin Hood Gate car park and walk downstream along Beverley Brook for about 500m until you reach the bridge to a metal gate letting onto the golf course. With your back to the bridge, walk towards the carriageway. The causeway is the old Mortlake-Ham boundary. Cross the carriageway and walk 75m up the rough track leading into Treebox Wood. On your right you should see a ditch and bank running off at an angle. This then runs up the northern edge of Treebox Wood, a few paces north of the treeline, and is traceable up to the brow of the hill.

The boundary along this stretch coincides with the northern boundary of Prior's Hill Copse, marked on Lane's map. The southern boundary of Prior's Hill Copse, incidentally may also be

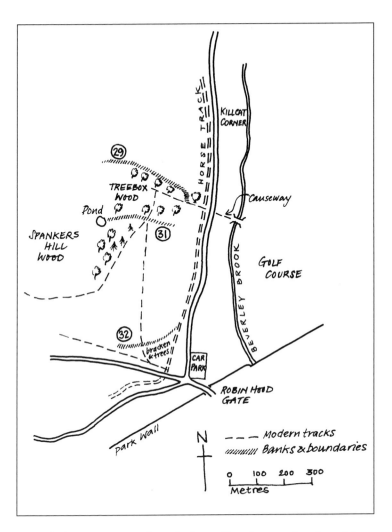

identified, since it runs along the line of bracken on the edge of the open greensward stretching back towards the car park (see sketch map), and may more or less be traced as a slight bank back to the edge of the round pond in Spanker's Hill Wood. While retracing your steps to the car park, the south eastern boundary of Beverley Close (also the perimeter of Hartleton Farm) is also identifiable as a low bank along the bracken/tree line on the south east corner of this open greensward.

3. KINGSTON's boundary with Ham changed substantially several times over the centuries and in 1994 the small remaining part was included within the Borough of Richmond.

4. The PETERSHAM-HAM boundary is almost impossible to follow, except approximately. But a large ivy clad ancient oak standing by the pond in the south east corner of the Sudbrook golf course (part of the original park) may be one of the old boundary oaks that ran almost straight up the escarpment and across to southern corner of the White Ash Lodge boundary fence, and then just a few paces west of the northern tip of the Upper Pen Pond.

11 The Isabella Plantation

Leave your car at the Broomfield Hill Car park.

Introduction

The final walk – especially if some of the longer walks proved a bit of a slog – is a well-earned leisurely stroll, ideal after a heavy Sunday lunch. There is no prescribed route, nor particular season for this unique woodland garden. It is most popular in April-May when the camellias, azaleas and rhododendrons are in bloom. But the show of colour can distract from the more satisfying quality of the garden, the interplay of shape, light and shade. Be guided by the map (p.110) and go where you will. Most of the delights, as in the rest of the park, are those of personal discovery. A brief history follows for those whose appetite for history remains undiminished, followed by the main garden features, a sketch map and a monthly listing of what to look out for.

A Brief History

The Isabella Slade was originally planted by Lord Sidmouth in 1831, with subsequent additions, first on the north east side in 1845, and then an enlargement of virtually the whole outer edge of the plantation in 1865. This planting was superimposed on some of the pre-enclosure oak pollards of Blacke Heathe (on Lane's map, p.10).

How it came by the name Isabella is unclear. It is possible it was named after the wife or daughter of a member of staff, but the name is at least 200 years old, appearing as 'Isabella Slade' on a map dated 1771. Lane's map shows the area was called The Sleyt (a slade was a greensward, open space between banks or woods, or boggy ground) in the early seventeenth century. Isabella may well be a corruption of 'isabel', which once meant a dingy or greyish yellow and would have referred to the colour of the sandy clay topsoil. The word has an unsavoury origin. In 1601 the Archduchess Isabella of Austria, Infanta of Spain and Governor of the Spanish Netherlands, vowed not to change her linen until Ostend had been recaptured from the Protestant Dutch. Never *ever* make a vow in the heat of the moment. The siege lasted for three years (1601-1604) and her counsellors must have faced the routine noxious ordeal of advising their unnecessarily malodorous governor. The name Isabel became a byword for grubby discolouration.

Prior to the development of Isabella Plantation in 1950, there was just a small pool (Still Pond) fed by a spring, and a muddy wallow at the foot of the slope in open parkland (now Peg's Pond). Both ponds, dug in 1861, were for the watering of livestock.

The present woodland walk is largely the inspiration of Wally Miller, head gardener and George Thomson, park superintendant, 1951-71, the former now immortalised with Wally's Island in Peg's Pond, and the latter with Thomson's Pond in the centre of the plantation and also with the wooden stumps that line the carriageways of the park, known as 'Thomson's teeth'. Thomson cleared the *Rhododendron ponticum* which is so widespread in the park and planted other Rhododendron species and also Kurume Azaleas around Still Pond.

The Main Stream running from Broomfield Gate was dug in 1960, the water initially pumped from the Sidmouth Plantation reservoir (visible behind the section of feather-edged wooden fence from Pembroke Lodge car park), and the Plantation enlarged to incorporate Peg's Pond. Since 1976 the water has been pumped from the Pen Ponds to feed each stream. A third stream was dug in the early 1980s through the wilder northern section, where the stream banks have been colonized by ferns, water plantains and brook lime.

THE MAIN FEATURES

The Heather Garden (G) was created in the open area outside the tree canopy. Some heathers are in flower virtually all the year round.

Still Pond acts as a dark mirror reflecting the azalea and rhododendron blooms in spring, and the *Acer Palmatum* (Japanese maple) foliage in autumn. It is also edged with *iris siberica*.

Thomson's Pond is edged with purple loose strife, sedges, irises and contains water lilies.

Peg's Pond contains tougher plants (the diving ducks wiped out the water lilies): flag iris, willow herb, sedge, water forget-me-nots.

The Bog Garden (I) is currently composed of three main plants: rushes which have completely displaced the previous bamboo, a grove of *Gunnera Manicata* (with enormous foliage) and *Osmunda regalis* (large ferns).

Acer Glade (M) is planted with nine different species of maples that provide spectacular autumn foliage and boast highly characteristic bark.

Wilson's Glade (N), named after Ernest Wilson the plant collector (see under *Azaleas* below), immediately to the right of Broomfield Hill Gate has already been planted with trees and bulbs, mainly introductions he himself made.

The pre-enclosure pollarded oaks (D) west of Still Pond are worth examining for their calloused hollow trunks, and the beef steak fungi that grow in them particularly in autumn.

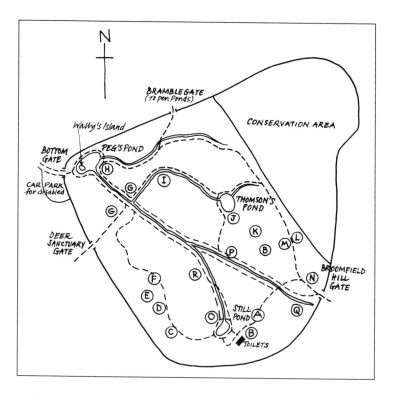

Multi-stemmed beeches grow in several parts of the garden. Their curious growth is something of an enigma.

The oak that grows in the embrace of a beech (O) is another curiosity to be found near the north west side of Still Pond.

THE FLORA

The garden is full of both common and rare plant species. Here are a few basic notes about some of the more notable species present.

Azaleas

The garden contains 15 known varieties of deciduous azalea. In addition the national collection of Kurume Azaleas (the 'Wilson

50') was started in the garden in 1991. These are the 50 evergeen azalea species assembled and made available in the West from 1919 onwards by the British plant collector Ernest Wilson, from 250 named kinds cultivated at the time in Kurume, Japan. (Incidentally, there is a local connection, for Coombe Wood, just outside Ladderstile Gate, was the nursery of the James Veitch who first commissioned Wilson to collect plants for him in China.)

Rhododendrons
There are 50 different species of rhododendron and 120 hybrids in the Plantation.

BIRD LIFE
It is sometimes forgotten that the good ground and tree cover makes the Isabella Plantation ideal for small animals, particularly birds.
Residents include redpolls, chaffinches, bullfinches, greenfinches, goldcrests, treecreepers, nuthatches, blue tits, coal tits, great tits, long tailed tits, dunnocks, lesser and greater spotted woodpeckers, as well as blackbirds, songthrushes, sparrow hawks and tawny owls. Waterfowl include plain and red crested pochards, tufted ducks, shelducks, pintails, moorhens, coots.
Visitors include perennials like the herons and other park residents and also
(i)   Spring: garden and wood warblers, redstarts, cuckoos, common and lesser whitethroats.
(ii)   Summer: blackcaps, spotted flycatchers.
(iii) Autumn: many of the above visitors, and also green sandpipers.
(iv)   Winter: siskins, kingfishers, reed buntings.

Butterflies in the Plantation include: Commas, Small Tortoiseshells, Wall Browns, Red Admirals, Peacocks, Meadow Browns, Speckled Woods, Small Heaths, Small Coppers, Purple Hairstreaks, Brimstones, Small and Large Skippers, Common Blues.

Dragonflies include Emperor dragonflies, Broad-bodied Chasers, Brown Hawkers, Common Darters and Golden Ringed dragon flies.

Damselflies include blued tailed, common blue and small red varieties.

WHAT TO LOOK OUT FOR EACH MONTH
January:
* By Broomfield Hill Gate (on right side of path) the Chinese Witch Hazel with fragrant yellow tassled flowers;
* Set back south of Acer Glade the Chinese *Mahonia bealei* shrub displaying yellow flowers with lily of the valley fragrance and *Viburnum tinus* (the Laurustinus) an evergreen shrub with white flowers; and also *Rhododendron dauricum* 'Midwinter' in rose-purple flower by Acer Glade path.
* At Peg's Pond the pollarded willow (*Salix alba*) with red and amber stems.
* On the north side of the Main Stream (P) two river birches (*Betula nigra*) one above the Heather Garden and the other nearer Broomfield Hill Gate.
* Set back below Camellia Walk (A), camellia 'J.C. Williams' with single pink flowers.

February
* On Camellia Walk (A) early Camellias include 'J.C. Williams', 'Mary Christian' and 'Wabisuke'.
* On the wet lawn (Q) near Broomfield Hill Gate early dwarf *Narcissus cyclamineus* with its long yellow trumpets and swept back petals.
* Below Still Pond *Rhododendron shilsonii* with deep red flowers. Other rhododendrons on the Main Stream, set back from Camellia Walk.

March
* Camellia Walk, several varieties in bloom.
* Set back in woodland west of Still Pond, *Magnolia mollicomata* (E), huge rose pink flowers.
* Above the Heather Garden on the Main Stream, *Pieris floribunda*, an evergreen shrub with drooping pitcher-shaped white flowers.
* Half way up the Main Stream, opposite Thomson's Pond, *Rhododendron lanigerum* with vivid red flowers.

April
* Along the streams marsh marigolds (*Caltha palustris*) and American Skunk Cabbage (*Lysichiton americanum*) with its yellow hooded spathes.
* Half way up the Main Stream *Rhodendendron emasculum*, thus named because the flowers lack stamens. Despite this apparently tragic deficiency, they make a nice rose-lilac mound of blossom. Further upstream *Rhododendron augustinii*, a blue-flowered species from China, and its hybrid form, *'Electra'*.

May

This is the month that most of the azaleas, rhododendrons and magnolias let rip. Apart from the display around Still Pond, the two beds of dwarf rhododendrons, *Rhododendron yakushimanum*, surrounded by its hybrids named after 'The Seven Dwarfs' (K) are worth seeing on the lawn south of Thomson's Pond. Look out, too, for the Pocket Handkerchief Tree (B), the flowers of which resemble hanging handkerchiefs. There is one south of Thomson's Pond which has just started flowering, and another on the eastern path from Camellia Walk to the toilets which is mature enough to flower any year now.

June

Apart from late flowering rhodondendrons and azaleas, look out for:

*   Along the streams, *Primula japonica*, in red, white and magenta forms, and also the Iris family: *ensate*, *sibirica*, and *pseudoacorus* (the native yellow flag iris).
*   Just above the confluence of the Main Stream and that from Thomson's Pond, *Stewartia pseudocamellia*, white camellia-like flowers, flaking bark.
*   Just above Still Pond the Snow-bell tree (*Styrax japonica*) with small bell-shaped flowers.
*   About 50 yards west of Still Pond, near the beginning of Beech Walk, a *Magnolia Sinensis* (C) in bloom.

July

*   In the south west corner of the Plantation, near Still Pond and Camellia Walk, late flowering rhododendrons.
*   Half way down Beech Walk, 'Swamp Honesuckle'(*Rhododendron viscosum*) with a spicy fragrance.
*   Thomson's and Peg's ponds are by now both frantic with dragonflies. Also on Thomson's pond Pickeral Weed's blue

flower spikes and tall spear shaped leaves.
* Along the streams varieties of the 'Day Lily' (*Hemerocallis*) in flower among the irises.

August
* On the lawn south of Thomson's Pond *Magnolia grandiflora*.
* At the southern end of Acer Glade a sweet pepper bush (*clethra*) with fragrant bell-shaped cream flowers.
* Along the streams native marginal plants, purple and yellow loosestrife, meadowsweet and greater willowherb.

September
* Near the wild stream through the north of the garden, *Hydrangea quercifolia* has papery panicles deepening into pink, and rough oak shaped leaves with bronze autumnal tints.
* Above Thomson's Pond, *Sorbus sargentiana* bears heads of small berries ripening to reddish-orange with red foliage, and nearby groups of the Guelder Rose (*Viburnum opulus*) with glossy red berries.
* A short walk down the main path from Broomfield Hill Gate, an unidentified magnolia bears large ovoid fruits like pineapples covered in curved spines.

October
* Near Thomson's pond, two *Nyssa sylvatic 'Tupelo'* trees turning brilliant scarlet; a group of shrubs 'Persian Ironwood' (*Parrotia persica*) amber, crimson and gold foliage.
* Close to Broomfield Gate, *Fothergilla monticola* with variegated fiery red and yellow foliage.
* Acers throughout the garden assume autumn tints.
* Above Still Pond the acer *Palmatum* assumes red foliage. On the left side of the stream running down to join the Main Stream is a tulip tree (R), its foliage now turning butter yellow.

November
* On the edge of Thomson's Pond, the Strawberry Tree (J) bears waxy bell-shaped pink flowers.
* Near the confluence of Still Pond Stream and Main Stream, *Camellia saanqua 'Rubra'*, with small single fragrant flowers.
* By Peg's Pond the Swamp cypress (*Taxodium distichum*) (H) foliage goes bronze in autumn.
* *Osmunda regalis*, the royal fern forms rusty clumps beside streams and ponds.

December
* By Broomfield Hill Gate, *Viburnum x bodnantese* shrub with fragrant pink flowers.
* By Peg's pond, pollarded willows with red and amber stems, and *Cornus stolonifera* with yellow/green stems under the nearby weeping willow tree.
* Above Thomson's Pond young birches with white stems, and east of the Pond *Prunus serrula*, mahogany red bark peeling in curly shreds.
* Throughout the garden acers with 'snake' bark. Look out for the Stinking Hellebore with its green flowers in the wilder parts of the garden.

Trees and Plantations

There are over 200,000 trees in the park. Many Dutch elms were lost in the 1970s, and over 1,000 trees were lost in the two great storms of October 1987 and January 1990.

The trees that are native to the park are essentially oak, ash, thorn and birch. Virtually all the others have been introduced.

OAKS

There are over 3,000 oak trees, over 40 per cent of the total number of parkland trees. Of these some 450 or so are 'pollarded', that is their upper branches have been lopped in order to produce a thick growth of young branches. They are also characterised by extremely thick trunks. All the oldest oaks in the park are pollards, and are most frequently found

(i)   along the Kingston-Petersham escarpment

(ii) in the remains of White Ash Lodge wood

(iii) near Robin Hood gate

(iv) south east of the Pen Ponds

(v)   on the east facing slopes of Spankers Hill and White Lodge hill

(vi) in lines of old hedgerows west of Bog Lodge

(vii) in High Wood.

Some of these trees date back to the fourteenth century, and may be part of the original replanting of timber on previously arable land (see Walk No. 2). Customarily pollarding first took place before a tree was fifty years old, and then once every seven years until it ceased to put out strong new branches. Some oaks were used to mark parish boundaries, but virtually none of these survive, and those which may have done are difficult to identify with any certainty. In the nineteenth century many more oaks were added,

The Shrew Ash before its partial destruction in 1875. Note the bar over which the sick child was passed. The woman may be a 'shrew mother'.

and in the 1920s many exotic varieties were also planted.

ASH

The finest specimens are in Isabella Plantation. The old Shrew Ash, north of Sheen Cross Wood, which was finally destroyed in the 1987 storm, has been replaced and the new sapling enclosed with a new iron fence. The old ash apparently grew on the boundary bank of Ashen Close, marked on Lane's map but scarcely perceptible on the ground. Despite its disappearance, the old Shrew Ash merits a note.

Reverence for the magical qualities of ash trees is recorded from early times in Britain and northern Europe, and these were often deliberately cloven. In his *Natural History of Selbourne*, Gilbert White gives an account of the supposed medicinal properties of the ash.

The Shrew Ash derives its name from the insertion of a live shrew into a hole bored into the trunk, which was then stopped up, as an antidote to sickness. The tree was still resorted to in the mid-nineteenth century as a source of cure for sick children and animals. A child was apparently cured by being passed nine times around a wooden bar wedged in the cleavage of the tree. This feat could only be performed by a 'shrew mother', a woman versed in the ritual and liturgy of the healing process. Sir Richard Owen observed several groups visit the tree before its partial destruction in 1875, and overheard some of the doggerel verse (sadly not recorded) used during the ceremony.

BEECH
There are only about 75 mature beeches in the park, mainly in Isabella Plantation. They were planted in the nineteenth century, as was the Beech Walk between Richmond Gate and Pembroke Lodge.

BIRCH
These are native to the sandy heathlands of the higher ground. Apart from Silver Jubilee clump planted near Richmond Gate in 1977, on the site of an old bandstand, they proliferate in Sidmouth Wood, Isabella and Pond Plantations.

HORSE CHESTNUT
These are almost exclusively in clumps of three to fifteen trees, planted in the mid-nineteenth century or later and were probably introduced as browse for the deer, who are extremely fond of 'conkers'.

LIMES
There are rows of limes in Petersham Park, and what may be early eighteenth century ones near the site of Old Lodge at the western foot of Spankers Hill.

RED OAKS
These may be found in clumps, the finest and oldest ones are south of the polo field. They were probably planted between the mid-nineteenth and early twentieth centuries.

SUGAR MAPLES
One hundred sugar maples, a gift from the federal government of Canada, were planted just above Gallows Pond in 1969. They marked one hundred years of diplomatic relations between the newly formed Dominion of Canada and Britain. It is no longer accepted policy to plant such exotic species in the park.

SWEET CHESTNUT
These may be found near Richmond Gate, around Sidmouth Wood, Treebox Wood, and lone trees in different parts of the park. They were probably introduced by Lord Sidmouth as browse for the deer.

THORNS
These have mostly been planted over the last hundred years. Many are so knarled as to give a misleading appearance of great antiquity. They live barely one hundred years.

WILLOW
The finest pollarded willows are on the banks of Beverley Brook, but note also the more ancient ones on Sudbrook.

Other species include wych elm, hornbeam, sycamore. Cedars of Lebanon and two other cedar species may be found in Petersham Park. Many exotic species, for example cherry, whitebeam, silver weeping lime, evergreen oak and balsam poplars were planted along the golf course boundary in 1922.

Plantations

There are very few parts of the park that have not been planted with trees at some stage. Many of the plantations listed below were clearly superimposed on previously treed areas. Barn Wood and High Wood, to name but two, have many mediaeval trees extant; Duchess and Sawpit woods were also mediaeval but thickened later. We also know from maps that Richmond-Sheen and Sheen-Roehampton belts and trees along the Thatched House Lodge portion of the escarpment existed before 1771, but may have begun to suffer depletion.

Dates of tree plantings:
(As you walk you may like to refer to the vintage of any woods you pass through)

Barn Wood	medieval
Beech Walk	c. 1840
Beverley Brook	1838
Broomfield Hill Plantations, West 1880, East 1878	
Conduit Wood	1829
Coronation Pltn (SE of Thatched House Lodge)	1902
Coronation Pltn (NE of Thatched House Lodge)	1953
Duchess,	eighteenth cent., possibly pre-enclosure
George Vth Jubilee	1935
Gibbet	1878
Golf course-Roehampton belt	1936
Ham Belt	1825-29
High Wood	medieval
Hornbeam Walk	c. 1834
Isabella Plantation, core 1831, 1845, edges 1865	
Jubilee Plantation	1887
Kidney Wood	1829

Killcat Corner   1864
King Clump (nr. Kingston Gate)   1901
Kingston Hill Plantation (along wall)   1826
Lawn Plantation   1883
Lower Pen Pond   1903
Pond Plantation   East 1824, West 1865
Prince Charles Spinney   1951
Richmond Gate Woods   1850
Queen Elizabeth Wood   1948
Queen Mother's Copse (NE of White Lodge)   1980
Roehampton Plantation (to Sheen)   1825
Sheen Cross Wood   1819
Sawpit Plantation   West 1873, East 1874
Sidmouth Wood North-east 1823, South-west 1830
Spankers Hill Wood,   East 1819, West 1824
Star and Garter Hill   pre-1850
Teck Plantation   1905
Tercentenary Plantation   1937
Treebox Wood (NE of Spankers Hill) 1877
Two Storm Wood   1991
Victory Plantation   1946
White Lodge Wood   North 1873, South 1879

The Deer

INTRODUCTION

There are about 400 fallow and 300 red deer in the park. They normally feed off grass, rushes, sedges, acorns, chestnuts, beech mast (or nuts), fungi, tree foliage, bark and grass and hay. the open landscape of the park is thanks to the voracious habit of the deer, clearing virtually all the cover from the ground and also creating a 'browse line' defining the base level of foliage on trees. During the winter months the deer receive a supplementary feed each night, feed being dispersed to each herd from the back of a moving vehicle, thereby ensuring that all deer have access.

Fallow males are called bucks and females does, but red deer males are called stags (or harts) and females hinds. New born fallow deer are fawns, but new born red deer are calves.

For about ten months of the year mature males of both species remain apart from mature females, calves/fawns and yearlings. Young males stay with the female herd until they are about 20 months old when they become mature and join the bucks or stags, but the mature females evict yearling stags for the duration of the rut, sometimes literally kicking them out.

FALLOW DEER: This is the most widely distributed of six species of deer in Britain. There is evidence of fallow deer in Britain before the last Ice Age, 150,000 years ago, but they became extinct. They were reintroduced in the historic period, and some thirty herds were recorded in the Domesday Book.

The park's fallow deer are of two types, menil and common. Both are coloured rich fawn with white spots in summer, but in winter the menil do not lose their spots entirely while the common fallow go dark fawn or grey and their spots virtually disappear. They may be distinguished in winter, the menil having a brown patch on their hindquarters and the common having a black patch on theirs.

RED DEER: The stags usually gather in groups of less than 20, with a dominance hierarchy based on age/strength. This hierarchy is usually established by gestures rather than overt threat. Higher ranking stags are likely to be 7-12 years old, carrying 13 or 15 point antlers or more (see below). In late September these groups break up as the stags go off singly in search of hinds. Red deer can live for up to 25 years, though by 1996 one hind had unusually reached the age of 27.

RUTTING. The rutting season for both red and fallow deer peaks in the last fortnight of October. Mating normally takes place at night but the pattern for fallow and red deer ruts is significantly different.

(i) Red stags round up as many hinds as possible in their 'hareem', migrate to a rutting area, and fight off challengers, a process of natural selection whereby hinds are impregnated by the strongest stags. The 'fights' are dramatic as stags lock antlers and seek to defeat their competitor in what are essentially trials of strength. It is unusual for stags to be hurt. By the end of the rutting season a red stag's antlers tips will be whitened from wear and tear in combat, and sometimes antler tips will be broken.

(ii) By contrast, fallow bucks wait for the does to come to them. They mark their rutting stands (roughly half an acre in size), scraping in the ground, and anointing the ground and trees with urine or rutty odour from their musk glands (below the eye) to attract does. They seldom keep a hareem. It is easy to locate the stands during or after rutting, for the areas are heavily scraped.

For example there are two stands just below the escarpment, one above Sudbrook Park, and another between Ham and Kingston Gates. Some of the rutting stands in the park are over a century old, successive bucks fighting to inherit the stand from their predecessors.

FAWNING: For both species gestation is 8 months, and within 20 minutes of birth a calf/fawn can walk, and in two days can run at the heels of its mother. Particularly soon after fawning, does (but not hinds) will signal danger by barking and 'pronking': bouncing stiff legged before running away. Hinds often return to the site of their own birth when calving. They can be aggressively protective during calving, and dogs that approach too closely may be attacked. Ham Cross Wood is particularly to be avoided in June.

THE CULL: Males are culled in August/September just before the rut, and females in November, just after it. About 200 deer are culled each year in order to keep the population stable, healthy, and with a good age structure, and the meat sold for market.

ANTLERS: In early spring, about 8 months after birth, lumps form on the pedicles, the permanent bony structures on the front of the skull from which the antlers grow. These are covered in 'velvet', the membrane that carries blood and oxygen for antler growth, which is shed in late summer when the antler is mature. The antlers themselves are shed annually in March. New antlers are soft, even slightly flexible. At 15 months a fallow male (technically known as a 'pricket') has unbranched spikes but thereafter grows 'palmate' antlers. With the red deer, the number of antler points (or 'tines') indicates age. The largest pair of antlers can exceed 12 points and can weigh 9kg, no less than half the weight of the skeleton. Very occasionally a 28 point deer will be seen in the park, an indication of the almost pampered life enjoyed in the park. The park record is a 29 point stag (sadly struck by a car and put down). In old age the antlers diminish each year in size and points.

DEER PENS: The primary purpose of deer pens was to provide supplementary feeding for deer, necessary with the larger herds in previous centuries. Two pens survive, a nineteenth century wooden enclosure north of the White Lodge and an open greensward on the edge of the deer sanctuary in High Wood, both worth looking at if you are passing by. Deer pens were surrounded by post and rail fencing with gaps wide enough for deer to enter but too narrow for cattle. Inside the deer pen would be a smaller enclosure that allowed only fawns in.

Fenced paddocks or pens would also be used by the keepers to catch deer, dogs being used to drive a selected animal into an opening which would be netted on the far side, where the deer would become entangled. An alternative method was to bring a deer to bay using hounds trained to seize it by the throat and ears and hold it down for the keepers to tie its legs. Today nets and hounds have been abandoned in favour of anaesthetic darts.

A SHORT HISTORY OF DEER IN RICHMOND PARK
Deer were first kept and fed in the 'Great Paddock' (now the golf course) on the east side of Beverley Brook. By the time of the 1660 Restoration there were some 2,000 deer, but within nine years Charles II was complaining that only 600 were left, partly the result of his hunting but more the result of thefts by park staff, particularly of the fawns.

During the eighteenth century there was a shift from hunting and killing to hunting and releasing deer. However, stags used for several hunts became aggressive, and deer hunting fell into abeyance in the second half of the century in favour of venison farming.

In 1831 Edward Jesse made a detailed survey of the deer, the first since 1669, by which time while there were 1,400 fallow deer there were only 50 red deer left. Intensive management and enlargement of the fallow and red herds took place, with gifts of deer from Earl Spencer and Lord Sidmouth, so that by 1850 there were 1,500 deer again. However, in 1871, a review of the cost of providing venison for the royal household established a cost per carcase in Richmond Park at £9.14s, an uneconomic cost. Rather than remove the herds, however,

> 'The Lords Commissioners considering the great addition which the presence of the herds make to the beauty of the Parks are not prepared to direct that they should be removed.'

In 1886 unusual behaviour among the fallow deer near East Sheen Gate was diagnosed as rabies, the first authenticated case in Britain. By September of the following year 264 fallow deer had been lost, but the epidemic was contained thanks largely to the fact that fallow herds are relatively static, and other herds in the park escaped the infection virtually unscathed.

The next peril for the deer was world war, when the demand for meat left the park with approximately 400 fallow and 50 red deer. With so many troops using the park it is a moot point how often bully beef tasted extraordinarily like venison.

Currently (1995) the fallow and red herds are about 400 and 300 strong respectively. About 20 to 30 deer are killed annually by motorists, and perhaps another 20 are attacked by dogs.

Birds

INTRODUCTION

Sixty years ago 133 different species of bird were listed as residents or visitors to the park. Remarkably, despite the enormous increase in people and dogs frequenting the park, there are still something in the order of 120 species to be seen. However, of these barely 50 are permanent residents, and the remainder are seasonal migrants and a handful of rare strays.

Of more interest perhaps is the changing balance of species. For example, the currently ubiquitous magpie could be described in 1937 as 'an occasional visitor to the park.....occurrences usually take place during the winter months.' A century earlier on the other hand Edward Jesse wrote of 'constant fights between the Mistletoe Thrush and the Magpie.'

Likewise there were only a few crows in 1900. A flock of 20 were worthy of mention in 1927 but a decade later one of 40 was not unusual. Unfortunately they have never looked back. They are a growing problem, living off high protein deer feed in winter and off animal waste throughout the year. They inhibit the proliferation of other species, raiding the nests of smaller birds. Thrushes of all kinds are now rarer than they were only a few years ago, and both house and tree sparrows once so common are now hardly seen at all. Skylarks, yellow hammers and redstarts have all declined as a result of the heavy dog presence. Nightingales were still plentiful a century ago in Sidmouth Wood, but now they have all gone. There are too many people. Because dogs must be leashed in it, the Isabella Plantation is perhaps the best place to look out for birds. (refer to the bird listing in Walk No. 11).

Birds to look out for in the park

There are a basic number of easily recognizable birds which will delight the eye.

* *Green Woodpeckers* (or Yaffles) are very common, particularly since they make an easy living from the anthills in the park.

* *Greater* and *Lesser Spotted Woodpeckers* are rarer, but can be seen in the Isabella Plantation, Sidmouth and Conduit woods. The Greater Spotted is easily detectable for the rapid hammerdrill sound of its beak. The Lesser Spotted, a nineteenth century introduction, was decimated by the winters of 1947/48 and 1962/63. Its population has still not fully recovered.

* *Kingfishers* may be seen on Beverley Brook, and on the Pen Ponds, and in the autumn in the Isabella Plantation, though they are shy and so swift in flight one may see nothing but a streak of electric blue.

* *Ring-necked parakeets*, escaped from captivity, may be spotted in the park, particularly along Beverley Brook. They are yellow-green and long tailed, with an orange-red half collar each side of the neck and a crimson beak.

* *Pheasants* and *partridge* are both occasionally released into the park. The cunning ones survive the foxes, but they are barely viable. Partridges are very occasionally seen in the bracken on the west side of Conduit Wood. Pheasants inhabit the Isabella Plantation where they are not hounded by dogs.

* *Herons* fish in most of the park's ponds. The heronry is in Pond Plantation on the south side of the Upper Pen Pond and may be observed from the north side of the Pond.

* *Cuckoos* seem to be reviving after being largely absent from the park for a number of years. The Isabella Plantation is popular. Their favourite nests belong to the dunnock, meadow pippet and reed warbler.

* *Kestrels* are easily identified as the only British birds of prey which hover over open ground. There are plenty around.
* *Sparrowhawks* are plentiful but harder to spot, since ambush is their stock-in-trade. They usually hunt in woodland clearings. With short powerful rounded wings, they can match the speed, twists and turns of their prey. Far easier to see than the bird itself is the remains of their prey, for they pluck their kill. Scattered feathers are a frequent sight on the ground, evidence that the sparrowhawk is alive and well in the park.
* *Tawny* and *Little Owls* are both found in the park. These are most easily spotted at dusk, when they begin hunting. Tawny Owls favour ancient pollarded oaks for nesting.
* *Waders* – for example, *sandpipers*, *ringed plovers*, *redshanks*, *greenshanks* and sometimes even *curlews* – can been seen on the Pen Ponds in spring and autumn, the best seasons for keeping an eye open for migrating birds.
* From April to August *swifts*, *swallows*, *house* and *sand martins* may be seen in the park. Their superlative flying may be enjoyed at the Pen Ponds where there are plenty of airborne insects for them to feed off.

Ponds

A number of natural water courses predate the enclosure:

(i)   The main one is BEVERLEY BROOK (which rises in Worcester Park) and its three feeders running down from Pond Slade, Sidmouth Wood and from the valley between Barn Wood and Sawpit Plantation.

(ii) SUDBROOK which drained the spring above Dann's Pond not far from Ladderstile Gate, down through the gully to Ham Dip, and thence through Ham Gate Pond to Sudbrook Park.

(iii) A STREAM, known in the nineteenth century as 'The Black Ditch', running north from Sidmouth Wood, through Conduit Wood to the park wall, being the boundary between Richmond and Mortlake.

In addition there were a number of springs, of which the most notable is the White Conduit in Conduit Wood, tapped in about 1500 for the Royal Palace. There were also a number of small ponds and one large one by Roehampton Gate, still in existence in the mid-eighteenth century. Other ponds, for example in front of the Old Lodge, and by Bog and Richmond Gates, came and went, as can be seen on John Eyre's map of 1754.

Most of today's ponds are either inundated gravel pits, or were specially dug to assist draining and provide water for the livestock. We do not know the precise dates when many of these were dug, but the following dates indicate the first mapped record:

Adams	1754
Barn Wood	1861
Bishops	1861
Conduit Wood	1861
Danns	1754
Gallows	1861

Ham Dip (or Glen)	1861
Ham Gate	1754
Leg of Mutton	1637
Martin's	1861
Peg's	1861
Pens	1746
Spanker's Hill	1754
Still	1861
Thomson's	1955
White Ash	1861

Leg of Mutton is the original pen pond (still known as such in 1876), and eighteenth century maps show the presently named Pen Ponds as 'The Canal'. All those ponds dug in 1861 represent part of the first effective attempt to deal with the widespread boggy areas in the park by Josiah Parkes, and to provide more adequate deer drinking facilities (Walk No. 7).

Index